Clinical Problem Solving

Clinical Problem Solving

Case Management

Norma S. Guerra

ROWMAN & LITTLEFIELD
Lanham • Boulder • New York • London

Published by Lexington Books
An imprint of The Rowman & Littlefield Publishing Group, Inc.
4501 Forbes Boulevard, Suite 200, Lanham, Maryland 20706
www.rowman.com

Unit A, Whitacre Mews, 26–34 Stannary Street, London SE11 4AB

British Library Cataloguing in Publication Information Available

Library of Congress Control Number: 2015949673
ISBN: 978-1-4422-4635-5 (cloth : alk. paper)
eISBN: 978-1-4422-4636-2

∞™ The paper used in this publication meets the minimum requirements of American National Standard for Information Sciences—Permanence of Paper for Printed Library Materials, ANSI/NISO Z39.48-1992.

Printed in the United States of America

Contents

Preface

The Listen-Identify-Brainstorm-Reality-test-Encourage (LIBRE Model) is a gentle problem-solving approach to processing challenges that have drained, leaving you feeling hopeless.

The text introduces problem-solving as a LIBRE Model approach to psychological, educational and/or counseling therapy. While real case examples have been included to explain the problem-solving case management in purpose and application, the confidentiality of these persons has been maintained. In practice, the LIBRE Model has been used for a variety of settings with equal number of roles. For example, the approach has been used for screening, diagnostics, research, personal and professional transitional development purposes as well as a primary or adjunct approach to therapy. Interested readers are encouraged to examine the literature related to these various uses for examples. The goal of this text is to provide a foundational case management approach (CMA) based on problem-solving. There is an exclusive advantage in approaching the client from a problem-solving view. Problem-solving provides a cognitive behavioral method and technique to identify and develop clients' goals toward self-regulated sustainable mental health. Problem-solving as a social cognitive behavioral exchange allows for a client-clinician partnership. The clinician's self-care prerequisite is unique in both self-regulation and modeling the importance of personal and professional wellness. Prior to providing client services, a clinician check-in to identify engagement investment is conducted and the clinician makes any engagement accommodations (calibrating personal engagement) to facilitate the client communication and counseling services. The problem-solving approach allows for clinical assessment of client's worldviews while providing the client a processing intervention to identified challenges.

Theoretically, the clinical problem-solving CMA is based on social cognitive, ecological, goal-oriented, and self-regulation theories as applied to client need. It is anticipated that you will be able to use this problem-solving approach in conjunction with other counseling and psychotherapy interventions. The LIBRE Model is a problem-solving activity which offers a structured framework for therapeutic interactions. Client data is collected with each problem-solving intervention to assess, monitor and gauge client progress. Within the text, we will step through the basics of how to prepare for the clinician role, the importance of maintaining an ongoing professional development plan (PDP) and preparatory procedures required for seeing clients, such as, when to use the problem solving model to collect client data, how to determine engagement styles for motivational monitoring and why it is important to demonstrate and document client change.

The text explains how to implement the problem-solving CMA. A client is followed, from entry up to the close of services, which includes the development of an individualized resiliency plan. All CMA documents created over the course of services provided are maintained within a case management portfolio (CMP), which will also be discussed. This Introduction provides an overview of the text and history of the LIBRE problem-solving Model.

The year was 2000. I received a call from my advocate friend and a community organizer. He shared the great gains that he had made within a high poverty level public housing complex. Under his leadership, they had established a food pantry, clothing store, study hall for the students, and sidewalk church for the children. I listened closely as he explained their inroads and encouraged him with the positive comment.

Within a short period of time, he began to describe the one missing service; we need a counseling model that can be trained and implemented within a brief period that will provide an immediate participant return. He explained that the people (clients) they were working with had many needs. He continued to detail the rallied workforce of professional mental health volunteers that had been invited to assist, I have counselors, social workers, pastors, and psychologists who are ready to work but we need to be trained with a common model that focuses all of these professionals on one page—how best to work with the people.

This call was a formal invitation. Will you come and train us? The remainder of the story was met with positive response and return. This was the impetus for the LIBRE Model problem-solving approach. It has continued to be applied to unique settings. For the last eleven years, it has been used as a CMA to support and transition teachers-in-training,

The many clients who have already been assisted by the LIBRE Model have come from diverse and multicultural backgrounds. Most have developed a new understanding of themselves as persons and as a result have worked through their daily life challenges. Over the years, common characteristics have been identified among those who have been successful with this approach. These requisites include: a normal range of cognitive and affective functioning; the willingness to explore change; and an expressed sense of being overwhelmed. This state of helplessness has often been expressed as feeling stuck. The acronym LIBRE (Spanish word for free) is used to introduce the five prompt problem-solving model. As I reflect on my friend's request, the LIBRE Model did provide a unifying approach for the volunteer professionals. The brief administration worked well with the high need community and it provided the clients an immediate and respectful return. The additional facet is that the LIBRE Model provides the clinician with an expectation that care for others begins with care for self, and this makes it a win-win approach to mental health services.

The LIBRE Model allows persons to express personal worldviews and possible resolution using their own words, reasoning, and context. As I recently heard it being described, the LIBRE Model is a gentle problem-solving approach to processing challenges that have drained you, leaving you feeling hopeless. The multifaceted task demand gives license for a social cognitive goal-oriented exchange. The problem-solving approach is strength-based, affirming client-focused method with an immediate resolution while providing the clinician insight into what the client defines as challenges and why the challenges are perceived to be so overwhelming. The client's responses to the five cues help the clinician structure how best to assist. The client's words and perspectives are the foundation in contextualizing the need and in the development of the intervention. To facilitate our understanding of how the LIBRE Model problem-solving approach works, I would like to introduce you to Leah. We met her in a school setting and we will refer to her throughout the CMA.

Leah is a sixteen-year-old first-generation US citizen. She is an attractive petite adolescent, junior in high school with plans to graduate next year. She loves to learn and takes great joy in pleasing her teachers, several of whom have become her mentors. They describe her as gifted and hope she will pursue college. As advocates for Leah, they believe that she will be a strong candidate for an academic scholarship. Leah's parents have dual citizenship, Mexico and the United States. They never attended school beyond the sixth grade, so they too are pleased that Leah has decided to remain in school. Leah's family has no long-term goals for her and Leah has no plans for herself beyond finishing high school, which seems to be a great ambition.

Although Leah has been doing well in school, she recently discovered that she is pregnant. Her parents told her they love her, but they will not allow her to live at home if she plans to continue seeing the father of her baby. They believe it is time for her to grow up and begin her life as a mother. Leah agrees with her parents. She understands that her parents want her to be self-sufficient and to take responsibility for her baby.

Leah decides to leave home. She and her boyfriend are very excited to be having a baby. She believes that they are ready to begin their life together. These recent changes have adversely affected Leah's school performance. She is experiencing a problem with absenteeism and her GPA has dropped, jeopardizing the probability of her finishing school. While her boyfriend quit school so she could finish school, her challenges continued. They spend very little time together. He now holds a steady job to provide for them, paying rent for their apartment and holding an extra part-time job at a neighborhood grocery store to pay for food and other expenses. In the meantime, her boyfriend's mother moved in with them. Leah was willing to accept her boyfriend's mother living with them since she promised to help with the rent, but mother has not been fulfilling her promise. To make the circumstances more complex, the mother's boyfriend is also living with them and neither of them are contributing to the rent or expenses. Leah feels this is unfair but, is unsure how to remedy the situation. Leah has never experienced these types intricacies in life.

Teachers stepped in here. While Leah could have asked for assistance (as a self-referral), in this case, her teachers submitted a referral to the counselor. The focus was Leah's absenteeism and drop in grades. The school provided counseling support. The clinical problem-solving CMA was implemented to initiate services. Figure 0.1 depicts is Leah's problem-solving LIBRE Model Stick Figure (LMSF), which was completed as a component of the clinical problem-solving CMA and used to introduce the mental health service model. The structure of the activity will allow Leah to address her concerns–her feelings, thoughts, and issues. The clinical process begins with this snapshot of what is on Leah's mind in-the-moment (of their meeting) and her problem-solving responses inform the clinician of Leah's perspective.

The LMSF, graphic organizer tool, is used to record her current needs. The stick figure design was created to help the client relax (even smile at the simple familiar stick figure shape). The client is asked to focus directly on her story as it recorded on the protocol form. Leah's recorded responses introduce the LIBRE Model product.

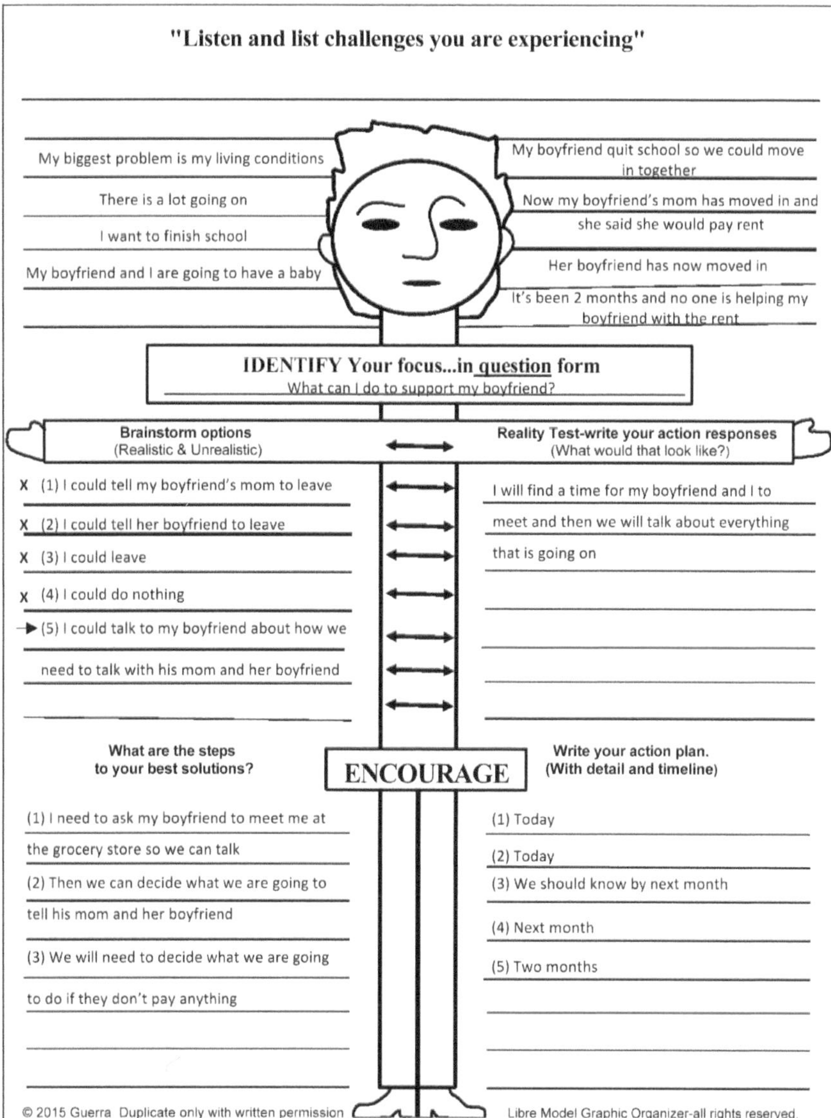

We can do this! We have options to move forward!

Figure 0.1 Leah's Recorded LIBRE Model Responses

Introduction

Much like an artist, we will first sketch (foundational theory), then line draw (as we examine the client and your role as clinician), and color (as we develop the case plan to meet needs) and shade in our work (with intervention and evaluation plans).

Objective: To provide a text chapter-by-chapter overview.

Mental health services are a social cognitive exchange involving a clinician and a client or in group therapy with a number of clients. Professional ethical boundaries and defined roles provide safeguards and intervention parameters. We will explore the clinical problem-solving CMA in application when addressing mental health concerns or when providing assistance with life problems. We begin with clinician wellness as the operational requisite to mental health services. The service provider's effectiveness is determined by self-regulated care in combination with training and experience. The CMA uses problem-solving to monitor and to manage the counseling. The CMA is used to identify the client need, to track progress, and to monitor clinician self-regulated investment.

As you develop your skills, this model will provide systems that can be used to track your clients' words, plans and actions toward their designed success. Case management includes self-regulation. You and your client will be expected to monitor your engaged investment. You will be asked to provide time for yourself to reflect upon the mental health services that you provide and the associated skills that you possess. This time will facilitate your affirmation of current expertise and allow you time to consider future professional development.

The CMA is based on ecological/contextual, social cognition, and goal-orientation theories. Each client session has a defined beginning, working middle processing time and closing period. You will find yourself teaching, modeling, providing interventions and experiencing these problem-solving tenets as you assist your client in moving toward resiliency. Continuous improvement and self-monitoring of mental health services are important. We examine how to develop a CMP, which is the client case folder used to structure and document the client's path toward resiliency and mental wellness. The CMA provides the counseling session structure used to introduce client growth and self-regulated positive change. As the clinician, it is your assessment that determines when and what additional counseling or psychotherapeutic interventions should be included. Collected CMA session data will help with these determinations and all CMA documents are kept within the CMP. Types of the information that will be collected include client achievements, failures, identified mental health goals, self-regulation and developing resilience strategies.

Let's begin. Each text chapter provides sequenced information that builds onto the next presentation. The theoretical underpinning provides background information about problem-solving as an informal clinical assessment and sets the stage for the CMA. Much like an artist, we will first sketch (foundational theory), then line draw (as we examine the client and your role as clinician), and color (as we develop the case plan to meet needs) and shade in our work (with intervention and evaluation plans). The LIBRE Model problem-solving activity is (the brief therapeutic intervention that will be used to identify need and gauge change) the paintbrush; it is a primary tool to set the development of this art into action.

The CMA implementation works with an established partnership between you and the client. The client uses the problem-solving to identify challenges and to develop resolutions. You in turn, listen, use Socratic questions and record your client's words and observed behaviors. Together, you and the client will specify the goals that will then lead to the intervention plan. These goals should address the referral and the client's identified needs. The first CMA step begins with the clinician's self-assessment. As a clinician, you want to identify your engagement style prior to each counseling session. Why, you ask? There is an inherent need to be self-aware and self-regulated. If I am unaware of my motivational attentiveness, how will I then gauge and examine the close-to-client affiliation required for an effective counseling working relationship? For example, what if I am more attentive than my client but I am not aware of self- and over-investment? This may likely impact the counseling services I offer. The counseling working relationship involves an interactive engagement that extends beyond rapport, requiring a delicate balance of being close without overstepping safety boundaries to introduce risk. This is a learned self-regulatory clinician skill; as such, I must be aware of my motivational investment so it does not overshadow that of my client.

For a novice clinician, executing this counseling social exchange can be somewhat intimidating. Maintaining a close working relationship without introducing an inappropriate relationship that is too close can be difficult. Compounding this challenge is the fear of what to expect. This is the first time you will meet the client—there is an inherent dread filled with questions: what if this person sees me as unskilled or I run out of things to say or ask. For experienced service providers, this skill has likely been learned the hard way—often through painful supervisory feedback indicating either that you did not establish the required empathy to develop a working relationship or that you became too involved with the client. Supervisory feedback may include comments like—you presented yourself as a friend rather than as a clinician (e.g., what were you thinking?).

With the CMA, engagement styles are identified prior to seeing each client. Clinicians make the appropriate engagement style adjustment (calibration) to meet the client's needs. Through the CMA, clinician and client engagement styles are addressed and monitored as the combination of initial and sustained attention. There are four gradient engagement investments that are tracked from the beginning to the close of the problem-solving task. Not all investment is the same. Engagement styles vary from no investment—potential to total investment—actual. Client productivity can be maximized by addressing (client and clinician) engagement styles. A self-regulated actual engaged clinician would be more efficient in addressing and monitoring client growth when compared to a potential engaged clinician. The clinician's self-managed engagement becomes the foundational preparation to meeting the client and addressing the client's needs.

The second CMA stage involves the referral and client preparation. Client information is framed within social, cognitive, cultural, and behavioral contexts. These elements are measured and monitored throughout each counseling exchange. Data is collected prior to seeing the client, in session and after the session ends. Evidence-based research with specific individual groups are referenced. A bank of questions are created and used in session with the client to better understand the client's unique situation. All interventions are framed with this larger context in mind.

Third, this is the first client session. The LIBRE Model problem-solving activity is administered to collect client information. Only the client's words are recorded. This information is then used to structure the client's intervention. The CMA establishes a beginning point, working middle period, and a closing point for both the client and clinician. The LIBRE Model problem-solving activity will be used strategically to record client problem-solving changes. Given its assessment qualities, it may be used as often as the counselor deems appropriate.

Fourth, involves the data analysis and case plan generation. Review of collected problem-solving units of information makes-up the fifth component. Sixth is the intervention and seventh involves the intervention evaluation; each component is developed prior to providing services. Services are then ready to be provided and monitored. Eighth, the CMA closes by providing the client a personalized resilience plan that is contextualized to meet the client's social cognitive and cultural goals framed within the client's ecological system as it has evolved. This plan is developed and implemented as an ongoing investment to measure gains. The client is given the opportunity to see progress that has been made and tracked through the problem-solving LIBRE Model exchanges. The client learns that self-regulation can be monitored through problem-solving and that in using problem-solving to address future challenges, there is a greater likelihood to achieve continued success. The client leaves the counseling with a tool that can be used in other settings.

The text begins with the Case Management Approach (chapter 1) used to structure the counseling services. The application of the LIBRE Model and LIBRE Model Stick Figure Tool (LMSFT) and protocol are outlined. In this chapter, it is also discussed how to use the results to conduct the client needs assessment, identify engagement styles, and develop a case plan to meet need(s) and intervention plan. Client monitoring through problem-solving checkpoints is also discussed. Bandura's core human agency properties are discussed within the context of problem-solving to provide the counseling theoretical structure. Service provider parameters and limitations involved in delivering direct and indirect services are presented. Ethical considerations and boundaries are examined in working with a client. Parameters examined include client safety and when to report.

The LIBRE Model is a core component of the CMA approach and it is strategically used to collect client information (chapter 2). The theoretical foundation is presented as background information. Bandura's[1] core properties of human agency and social cognitive theory are explained as the mechanisms for sociocultural and behavioral change.[2] Vygotsky's[3] Zone of Proximal Development (ZPD) is examined in the context of problem-solving support. Bronfenbrenner's[4] ecological-systems theory and later work with bioecological systems based on Bronfenbrenner and Morris[5] are discussed as ecological context. The CMA is attentive not only to what clients say, but also how they say it. Rogoff explains, "cognitive development consists of coming to find, understand, and handle particular problems."[6] Finally, exercises have been provided at the close of most chapters to provide practice.

We then look closely at the CMA components. Beginning with the service provider who will also be referred to as a clinician. The Clinician: Service Provider (chapter 3) discusses the implications of clinicians' communications with clients. Directions include setting the context for services, defining the level of services to be provided and monitoring client change. The text client (Leah) is revisited to illustrate the referral intake and it is used throughout the text as a reference point to observe the new and developing skills in application.

You will be asked to consider your own professional strengths and vulnerabilities in providing mental health services. This personal preparation is the first facet of professional development in client preparation. The details involved in receiving a referral, whether it is a self-referral or an outside agency referral are discussed. Preparing background questions is important and should include social, cultural, cognitive, and emotional aspects.

The Referral and Client Preparation (chapter 4) addresses how best to use the intake information to organize the first session and how to begin developing background questions that may be introduced with subsequent sessions. The details of how to introduce each session are presented. The relations between the CMA counseling session activity and document maintenance within the CMP are discussed. Practice client exercises will be introduced throughout the text.

Chapter 5 addresses the First Client Session: LIBRE Model[7] with the LMSF, which was presented within the Preface of the book is explained in detail. The text client is referenced to illustrate the problem-solving application. LIBRE is an acronym for the five steps of the problem-solving process:

L—listen
I—identify
B—brainstorm
R—reality-test
E—encourage

Clinicians are taught how to administer and record client responses. The LMSFT is the graphic organizer that accompanies the problem-solving exchange. The LMSF tool also functions as a clinical protocol to record the problem-solving responses. Each time the LIBRE Model is presented, the ethical ground rules are used to set-up an environment that is respectful and safe, where confidentiality is maintained and where there is a sense of free independence and openness to speak. Several tables and graphics are provided, along with a copy of the LMSF.

Beyond the LIBRE Model administration, this chapter examines the components of the data content collected from the exchange. Instructions are provided on how to score the LMSF.[8] The next three chapters (chapters 6–8) outline Data and Analysis and Case Plan Generation: Clinical Problem-Solving, Engagement Styles, and Promoting Client Growth and Development.

The problem-solving-activity is explained. Rubrics for identifying engagement styles and initial and sustained attention are included to assist clinicians. Considerations and instructions are presented for how best to incorporate the collected data into the case plan. The case conceptualizing or as sometimes referred to as the outline of services and plans, is discussed. Scoring worksheets and tables are included, along with several graphics. The Review of Collected Problem-Solving Units of Information are presented and explained.

The Intervention: Promoting Client Growth and Development chapter integrates social values information with lifespan needs into the development of the client assessment plan. The discussion shifts attention to the importance of social cognitive human growth and development across the lifespan using Erikson's[9] theory to contextualize the processing of psychological crises. Erikson's eight stages of development include: working with children (stages 1–4), adolescents (stage 5), young adults (stage 6) and older adults (stages 7–8). Each section addresses strategies and activities for introducing social cognitive self-regulated skills. Vygotsky's[10] work with the ZPD is referenced to introduce the importance of scaffold assistance to learning. Bandura's[11] social cognitive learning theory is used to frame the client's interaction with self as influenced by the environment, which in turn mediates goals and plans. Socratic questioning is discussed and used to summarize key concepts presented throughout the text along with open-ended and self-reflective questions.

The Intervention Evaluation: Managing Change and Crisis Situations (chapter 9) addresses change, such as a crisis, which may be acted out in anxiety, depression, and/or other affective states. Social cognitive implications of risk are discussed, including symptoms and treatment options for identifying and developing intervention strategies. Risk is examined in relation to the client's cultural, social cognitive, and chronological experiential age. Problem-solving is presented as the tool for monitoring and introducing self-instructional approaches. The chapter includes safety plans, when to report, and how to optimize safety. While an earlier chapter addressed boundaries from an ethical lens, this chapter focuses on client safety and support and the importance of working with formal and informal client communities.

The CMA closes with the Resiliency Plan: Developing Resiliency through Self-Regulation. Chapter 10 examines Skinner and Pitzer;[12] Appleton, Christenson and Furlong;[13] and Fredricks, Blumenfield and Paris[14] work with resiliency are presented in terms of engagement and self-determination theory. The clinician and client create the customized resiliency plan. As the client develops more personal management skills in making decisions and processing challenges, the clinician works with the client to develop strategies that encourage resiliency. The role of protective factors (support systems) and how these may be used to develop resiliency in maintaining sustainable change.

The CMP (chapter 11) discusses the client case folder. The CMP is the document home for the client's social cognitive and counseling developmental recorded changes. The CMP includes: experience notes, listings of gains, challenges, and recommendations. Engagement style information is maintained within the CMP. The CMP has two purposes: (1) to maintain a reference for the clinician and (2) to provide the client referenced documents of change. For example, the client may be provided engagement patterns to learn how to monitor self through personal problem-solving. Thus the CMP provides the provision for self-monitoring to be introduced.

The Working under Supervision (chapter 12) presents the LIBRE Model problem-solving structure when working with supervisees. The goals of the supervisory process are presented in the context of the problem-solving, which has the clinicians' expressed philosophical and professional goals to monitor professional success. Supervisors are presented with information concerning the tracking of client gains. This allows the supervisor to provide the supervisee feedback on multiple levels. In addressing client management, the supervisor is able to follow the clinicians' cases as evidenced in services provided and client problem-solving experiences. Client LIBRE Model responses provide the supervisor a view of the case managed services received. Similarly, the service provider is able to address personal and professional challenges and changes within the structural support of the LIBRE Model.

The Engagement Styles in Consultation (chapter 13) addresses the importance of defining the roles and expectations of professional service. Consultative and indirect services are defined. Roles, service boundaries and clarifications that define the consultation must be established, along with strategies for meeting the defined services. Considerations about how best to coordinate consultative or indirect services are discussed. The LIBRE Model is presented as a means to structure services.

The Reflection: Sustaining Success (chapter 14) discusses the importance of monitoring change in the context of social and cultural success and working within nonsupportive systems. Collecting and managing formative and summative feedback is discussed in reference to identity development based on Bandura's[15] human agency four core properties: intentionality—goal development and the plans to execute those plans; forethought—cognition associated with future goals and plan development; self-reactiveness—one's self-regulation of plans, thoughts, goals; and self-reflectiveness—one's self-efficacy in planning and execution. We end as we began with a professional development revisit and commitment to be the best service provider possible.

NOTES

1. Albert Bandura, "Toward a Psychology of Human Agency," *Perspectives on Psychological Science* 1, no. 2 (2006): 164–180.

2. Albert Bandura, *Social Foundations of Thought and Action: A Social Cognitive Theory* (Upper Saddle River, NJ: Pearson Education Prentice Hall, 1986).

3. Lev S. Vygotsky, *Mind in Society: The Development of Higher Psychological Processes* (Cambridge, MA: Harvard University Press, 1978).

4. Urie Bronfenbrenner, "Ecology of the Family as a Context for Human Development: Research Perspectives," *Developmental Psychology* 22, no. 6 (1986): 723–742.

5. Urie Bronfenbrenner and Pamela A. Morris, "The Bioecological Model of Human Development," in *Handbook of Child Psychology*, 6th ed., edited by William Damon and Richard M. Lerner (Hoboken, NJ: John Wiley & Sons, 2006), 793–828.

6. *Apprenticeship in Thinking: Cognitive Development in Social Context* (New York: Oxford University Press, 1990), 190.

7. Norma S. Guerra, "LIBRE Model," Unpublished Manuscript, (2001); Norma S. Guerra, "Revised LIBRE Model Stick Figure," Unpublished Instrument, (2005); Norma S. Guerra, "LIBRE Stick Figure Tool: A Graphic Organizer to Foster Self-Regulated Social Cognitive Problem Solving," *Intervention in School and Clinic* 44, no. 4 (2009): 229–233.

8. Norma S. Guerra, "LIBRE Model: Engagement Styles in Counseling." *Journal of Employment Counseling*, 44 (2007): 2–10; Norma S. Guerra, "LIBRE Stick Figure Tool: A Graphic Organizer to Foster Self-Regulated Social Cognitive Problem Solving," *Intervention in School and Clinic* 44, no. 4 (2009): 229–233.

9. Erik H. Erikson, *The Life Cycle Completed: A Review* (New York: W.W. Norton & Co, 1982).

10. Lev S. Vygotsky, *Mind in Society: The Development of Higher Psychological Processes* (Cambridge, MA: Harvard University Press, 1978).

11. Albert Bandura, "Toward a Psychology of Human Agency," *Perspectives on Psychological Science* 1, no. 2 (2006): 164–180.

12. Ellen A. Skinner and Jennifer Pitzer. "Developmental Dynamics of Student Engagement, Coping, and Everyday Resilience," in *The Handbook of Research on Student Engagement*, edited by S. Christenson, A. Reschly and C. Wylie (New York: Springer Science, 2012), 21–45.

13. James J. Appleton, Sandra L. Christenson and Michael J. Furlong. Student Engagement with School: Critical Conceptual and Methodological Issues of the Construct. *Psychology in the Schools* 45, no. 5 (2008): 369–386.

14. Jennifer A. Fredricks, Phyllis C. Blumenfeld and Alison H. Paris. School engagement: Potential of the concept, state of the evidence. *Review of Educational Research* 74 (2004): 59–109.

15. Albert Bandura, "Toward a Psychology of Human Agency," *Perspectives on Psychological Science* 1, no. 2 (2006): 164–180.

Chapter 1

Case Management Approach

The Case Management Approach is a mental health services shared partnership.

Objective: To examine the Case Management Approach (CMA) counseling structure.

Working a puzzle can be quite rewarding once you begin to see all of the pieces coming together. This CMA chapter provides that integrated view of services and documentation. Each CMA session has defined strategies, activities, and data collection provisions to facilitate and monitor change. This chapter will define CMA and show how it differs from other conceptualization approaches. Will discuss the CMA components:

1. Clinician self-assessment and calibration
2. Referral and client preparation, which includes clinician background work
3. The first client session: Administration of the LIBRE Model problem-solving activity
4. Data analysis and case plan generation
5. Review of collected problem-solving units of information, which includes client anticipated challenges, risks, and personal strengths conceptualized within the problem-solving experience
6. Intervention, which includes criteria addressed and selected counseling technique included
7. Intervention evaluation, which includes the measurement of the selected criteria and counseling technique implemented
8. Resiliency plan, which includes follow-up questions to develop and monitor self-managed resiliency

What is CMA? CMA is a social cognitive, cultural, and behavioral counseling exchange introduced to create a client-contextualized intervention that is measured and monitored toward positive self-managed change.

The CMA is a mental health services shared partnership. The clients are accountable for content of any problem-solving activity. Their investment is monitored as engagement to facilitate personal development. Clients are taught to problem solve and self-regulate personal change. The clinicians' self-assessment involves monitoring their own engagement. They calibrate their engagement (adjust their investment) to best assist the clients' needs. Clinicians function as guides and facilitators with different boundaries and roles from the client. For example, even if the clinician believes the client is wasting time venting, this judgment is never communicated. Opportunities are sought to analyze and introduce other means for processing challenge and any affect. The client's engagement is monitored to gauge investment toward self-managed change.

How does the CMA differ from other approaches? The CMA conceptualization is markedly distinct, first with the roles of the client and clinician and second, with the ongoing counseling self-reflection used to develop the client's resiliency plan. The CMA is designed to protect and call attention to mutual self-regulated client and clinician investment so that the counseling exchange is managed and protected by both parties. The clinician's roles include: guiding, facilitating, monitoring, reality-test and teaching the client new skills.

What are the CMA components? The CMA components include: (1) clinician self-assessment, a personal calibration that involves the clinician's engagement accommodation to meet the client's needs; this exercise is completed each time prior to seeing the client, (2) referral and client preparation, which includes the clinician's attention to the client's background information provided; this information addresses the client's cognitive, cultural, and chronological age (3Cs) data, the client's social cognitive human development, and any prior cognitive and/or behavioral experiences reported, (3) first client session, which includes the administration of the problem-solving LIBRE Model, (4) data analysis and case plan generation (5) review of collected problem-solving units of information, which is then combined with the referral and background information; these units of information are analyzed to craft the case plan, (6) intervention, which is then developed to set the service direction, (7) intervention evaluation that is developed to measure and track change, and (8) resiliency plan that is developed with the client to monitor gains that have been made and strategic support to address future challenges. Follow-up questions are used to monitor the case plan and anticipated challenges and risks. Client strengths are incorporated into the client's self-managed resiliency plan (see Table 1).

Table 1.1 Presentation of the Case Management Approach Form

Client Case Management Approach	
Clinician Engagement Session 1 Session 2 Session 3	Client Engagement Session 1 Session 2 Session 3
Engagement/Content L I B R E	
Background Information Referral Additional Questions:	
3 Cs Culture-	Additional Questions:
Cognition-	Additional Questions:
Chronological Age-	Additional Questions:
Social Cognitive Human Development Additional Questions:	
Intervention Plan:	

How do we implement the CMA? To illustrate the CMA application, let's return to our text client Leah, and I will walk through the CMA sequence as the clinician who has received the referral to work with Leah.

Clinician Self-Assessment: Service Provider

1. While the details of how to assess engagement styles will be presented in chapter 7; for this example, I will summarize the process. The problem-solving activity is completed. Based on the problem-solving responses, initial and sustained attention are determined. Thus, my problem-solving performance, which includes specificity and content investment from the beginning to the close of the activity, supports my self-assessment that my engagement style is that of actual engagement. I further determine that this is an appropriate engagement style to enter the first session. My engagement style is recorded on the CMA form.

Referral and Client Preparation

2. Review the referral (self-referral) and background information. I evaluate the provided referral information and data collected from Leah's teachers.

I analyze the content and begin to generate questions that I will address with her. For instance, is Leah's current challenge the same as the school's recorded referral challenge? Does Leah's family see Leah's behavior as a challenge? What kind of relationship does Leah have with her family?

Assess 3Cs. (1) Culturally; I develop questions about her familial culture. If I have limited information about her culture, I use this as my invitation to conduct research. In this case, I want to better understand the traditional Mexican-American culture. I must have a working knowledge of the culture to be able to determine if her current behavior is consistent with her cultural values. Is her recent academic performance in school related to something occurring at home? What are the home values in relation to school? After speaking with her teachers, I learn she has not been attending school regularly. (2) Cognitively, Leah is functioning well at school; she is reported to be at grade level. Further, until this challenge arose, she was on a direct academic track for graduation. I develop questions about how she sees herself as a student. Questions may include: do you consider yourself smart? Do you like to learn new things? What's your favorite subject? (3) In reference to chronological age, she is a high school student with an on-grade-level history of academic success. Questions may address what has happened to create the change in behavior. Such as, when did you first notice that your grades began to drop? Was the material covered in class too difficult to understand? Did you find yourself distracted in class?

Determine the social cognitive human development. Behavioral changes are also noted. Something appears to have occurred within Leah's social cognitive environment. For example, change in living conditions. Develop questions about her social cognitive development. Questions that may be introduced include: Do your parents give you the freedom to go and come as you wish? Have you always had this freedom or did the freedom occur with your sixteenth birthday? Do you have any home responsibilities—for example, caring for younger brothers or sisters; cooking dinner? Do your parents work in the evening? Do you work after school?

First Client Session

3. Meet with the client and administer the LIBRE Model. I meet with Leah, introduce myself, and explain my role and the session parameters. I explain the referral and ethical ground rules (confidentiality and reportable boundaries) and explain that I will come with an activity each time we meet. I ask her if she has any questions. She indicates no. Rather than beginning with the prepared questions, I ask if she would be willing for us to complete a problem-solving activity so I can get to know her better, even as we address what is going on in her life. My rationale for beginning with the problem-solving-activity is to explore with her the challenges she defines (apart from those defined within the referral). She agrees. I record all of her responses and review her plan with her (see Preface for the completed LMSF with Leah's responses). One final thought about beginning with the problem-solving activity, depending on the results of the problem-solving, I am always ready to introduce my prepared questions.

Leah's plan had no overt personal risk so the counseling guidance addressed contingencies with the expectations of her plan. We agree to meet the following week to discuss the implementation of her plan, which includes talking with her boyfriend. She tells me that she will let me know how her talk with her boyfriend goes. I thank her for her time and let her know that I will be here next week to see her. We close and she returns to class.

I annotate that she appears to have moved beyond her chronological age into the social cognitive young adulthood stage of development (Erikson's stage of Intimacy). Leah appears to be finding herself with another new family. She indicates that she wants to be in this evolving close interactive relationship rather than remaining alone. Leah also states that she has never encountered this type of challenge before. This response is recorded as normal for a teenager. Her decision to live with her boyfriend and move away from her parents seems to support the young adult social cognitive development. In terms of affect, Leah did not express any distress. This would suggest that she sees living with her boyfriend as the next step in her life.

She is clear about her challenges and goals. She provides a detailed plan that is within her control. She explains that she needs to talk to her boyfriend. This is Leah's resolution plan to her identified concern. I will address this decision with our future meeting and use her feedback as a means to measure her accountability to herself. In addition, given the specificity and detail in the problem-solving responses (initial and sustained attention), I identify her as exhibiting an actual engagement style. I note that I will need to make sure that I enter into each of our sessions using the same actual engagement style; thus, matching her style.

Data Analysis and Case Plan Generation

4. In developing the case plan, I propose meeting with both the referring agency (school) and Leah (as the client) to identify a need (see Table 1.2). As much as possible, try to match the client's need with the referral need. I make sure that the referral, client need, and collected data are reflected by the case plan. In Leah's case, the school referral was focused on grades, attendance, and Leah's graduation suggests a lack of focus. Leah's focus is on her new living situation, she is concerned about housing needs (boyfriend's mother and paying rent) and the unborn baby suggests a lack of support. The proposed case plan may include (from the referral) a lack of self-management or time-management skills and (from her problem-solving) a lack of support. Thus, the intervention may involve teaching Leah problem-solving skills so that she will be able to ask for the time management (school referral) and personal support (personal identified need) that would allow her to address school and outside school concerns.

Review of Collected Problem-Solving Units of Information

5. Analyze the LIBRE Model content and determine the engagement style. The content supports the assumptions I have made about Leah's cultural background based on the referral. She is attentive to her immediate environment and is willing to process her challenges. In reviewing the content, I note that she is experiencing some cultural challenges as evidenced in her statement that she had to choose to stay with her parents and raise her child without a father or leave home to live with her boyfriend and raise their child together. I also note that as per the initial referral, she has had cultural success within school—I record this as a positive academic cultural experience. In analyzing her identified challenge, I note that it is different from that reported within the referral. She does indicate self-awareness and acknowledges that she is not doing well in school, but her living conditions hold the most important challenge for her.

Intervention

6. I address what I believe will be anticipated challenges, anticipated risks, and anticipated strengths. An anticipated challenge is associated with learning a new skill. Leah has shared that she has never solved problems in the manner presented during our meeting. Until she feels comfortable with the skill, she may be inclined not to use it. An anticipated risk is that she may become overwhelmed as she attempts to please everyone within her social context. Even as she learns to problem solve, this will not make her decisions easier. I identify client strengths next, which include her awareness of her environment and willingness to create a positive change. Additional resources (strengths) identified are her teachers and parents, who appear to be ready to assist as needed.

Leah's intervention plan will include learning how to problem solve. In speaking with the referring agent, we determine that four meetings will be conducted to assist Leah.

Session one: Begin with the scripted introduction to the session; we revisit the current problem-solving plan Leah created. The plan is to have a follow-up discussion about her resolution plan; we review the steps to the problem-solving process, and I answer any questions. Then, Leah practices completing another LIBRE Model problem-solving exchange. I will ask only the generated questions that will help Leah learn how to problem solve.

Session two: Begin with the scripted introduction and review any new proposed resolution plans. Check in to see how she is doing physically, how she is doing in school, and how she is adjusting to her new living situation. We discuss the importance of self-attentiveness (taking time to attend to her needs), self-regulation and discuss what each may include. Assuming a therapeutic guiding role, we talk about where she sees herself and how she is managing the changes that are occurring. I introduce questions that assist her in developing criteria for self-reflection and self-management. Clinical homework will include practicing self-regulation.

Session three: Begin with the scripted introduction and check-in. Leah is asked about her prior problem-solving plans. We discuss what worked and what didn't work and why. Leah completes a third problem-solving activity without assistance. I explain that next week will be our last session, and I ask her to begin thinking about the type of support she will need to be successful in the future. We role-play what that might look like and identify people within her environment who would be willing to provide support.

Session four: This will be the final meeting with Leah. Begin with the scripted introduction and check-in. Progress will be reviewed and Leah will again address what worked and what did not. She will review her three prior problem-solving activity stick figures and be asked to identify common factors that worked from week to week as well as those that did not work. I'll revisit the importance of self-regulation, asking her for examples of how she self-regulates. We will discuss who within her current school and family are available to assist her if she runs into a problem. I make a commitment to contact the identified school staff so that she will have someone who will listen if she needs to talk. Finally, the session closes with Leah completing a fourth problem-solving activity to address future anticipated challenges.

Intervention Evaluation

7. Evaluation criteria and measures. Each session has a specific plan with evaluative measures generated for each. The evaluation plan developed for Leah is as follows:

Session one: This session will be evaluated using each one of the problem-solving steps as specific skills: (1) Was she able to List items of concern? (2) Was she able to Identify one concern that was within her own control to process a resolution? (3) Did she Brainstorm possible and impossible solutions? Was she able to eliminate improbable solutions? Was she able to prioritize the remaining options? (4) Did she Reality-test remaining options? Was she able to articulate what would occur if she acted on her proposed options? (5) Was she Encouraged creating a plan with a timeline? I would expect a 60 percent (three prompts) success rate with this first practice. If not, I will assign homework and practice with her within session two.

Session two: I will observe her understanding of self-regulation with the examples she provides, anticipating that she will be able to provide two distinct examples of self-regulated behavior. With the practice problem-solving, I would anticipate 70 percent or four of the prompts to be correctly completed.

Session three: Each one of the problem-solving steps will be evaluated as specific skills: (1) Was she able to List items of concern? (2) Was she able to Identify one concern that was within her control? (3) Did she Brainstorm possible and impossible solutions? Was she able to eliminate improbable solutions? Was she able to prioritize the remaining options? (4) Did Reality-testing occur? Was she able to articulate what would occur if she acted on her proposed options? And (5) Was she Encouraged to create a plan with a timeline? I would expect a 100 percent (five prompts) success rate with this practice. The redundancy in the evaluation is intentional to reinforce skill development and self-efficacy.

Session four is the final session: I will look for demonstrated self-regulated awareness. This skill will be demonstrated with the language she uses in talking about herself and her current situation. For example, she may say I really want to do this, but I won't because it will not accomplish what I want to accomplish. In terms of the problem-solving decision-making, I would anticipate 100 percent correct completion as demonstrated in this well-rehearsed activity. Of course, if the 100 percent is not achieved, I will work with the school to provide the ongoing instruction and support so that this life skill is learned and internalized as an option for addressing current and future problems.

Resiliency Plan

8. Follow-up questions are used to monitor change toward self-managed resiliency. Follow-up questions will be addressed at each session. The evaluation criteria and measures are used to monitor change. The identified supports are added to the developing resiliency plan. Next steps and recommendations are offered to the referral agency. In Leah's case, I identified a teacher who Leah said she enjoyed visiting with. This teacher will be contacted and made available to her should she need someone to share her problem-solving and thoughts with. Leah and I talk about protective factors, for example strong character qualities that students may want to consider in making friends. We develop a resiliency plan that allows Leah to practice caring for herself with the needed support to maintain the gains that she has achieved.

What does the CMA documentation include? The CMA contains the responses to the eight items listed above. Each is systematically addressed to confirm and support the intervention. The resiliency support plan is also a CMA document.

Why are follow-up questions continually being developed over the entire CMA exchange? Open-ended questions are invaluable to gather data that will facilitate the intervention services provided. Preparing questions ahead of time helps anticipate client need. The 3C (culture, cognition, and chronological age) questions are used to confirm notions you may have about the client. By continuing to develop questions, you will always have them ready for use. The purpose of the follow-up questions is to introduce new ways of thinking and processing change. Questions can be used to challenge and examine thoughts. Beyond the questions, role-play and narrative scenarios can be developed to practice new emerging skills.

One important consideration: maintaining a list of questions does not mean that you will ask all of the questions. You may decide to ask several during each session. You may decide to use the questions as homework for your client or the questions may become your homework as you prepare for the client. There may be times when you decide to never ask the questions that you have generated. Why then is it important to generate a list of questions, you ask. Early on we discussed the importance of understanding the client,

Table 1.2 Case Management Approach Form—Resiliency Plan

Individualized Treatment Plan: Anticipated Challenges: Anticipated Risk(s): Anticipated Strength(s):	
Intervention Plan	Evaluation
Resiliency Plan – Next Steps and Recommendations	

what that client's background may include and the client's worldview, questions help to explore these topics. The questions become the content that you bring to the session. Questions may also become teachable moments as the client considers the responses. Interventions and skills development, practice role-play, and other social cognitive activities may also come from questions generated; however, your client may also introduce new information that would make your questions irrelevant. It is important for you to listen and adjust accordingly. For example, I may prepare a number of questions about Leah's relationship with her boyfriend. However, if with our next meeting Leah decides to move back home and not remain with her boyfriend, asking questions about the boyfriend and their relationship may not be appropriate.

See yourself in an investigative role. Use the questions to facilitate how best to support your client. Come prepared with questions to facilitate the communication and come also with an activity based on the questions that will build to that targeted skill. Listen and watch the client closely, gauge your activity to encourage and support. Allow the client the time to process and reflect upon the new skills introduced.

Summary

The CMA provides the infrastructure for your counseling services; begin with yourself in accountability to your clients. Self-regulate to adjust and focus your skills, thus better assisting your clients while helping yourself to monitor any potential over or underinvestment. The CMA includes:

1. Clinician self-assessment
2. Referral and client preparation
3. The first client session
4. Data analysis and case plan generation
5. Review of collected problem-solving units of information
6. Intervention
7. Intervention evaluation
8. Resiliency plan

Practice Client Exercise

You have received a self-referral, a twenty-seven-year-old client. Minimal information has been provided. Reference the eight CMA stages to develop background questions that should be considered in the development of your plan.

Chapter 2

LIBRE Model Clinical Problem-Solving Theoretical Framework

The importance of theory to practice cannot be overstated.

Objective: To study the theory that supports the Listen-Identify-Brainstorm-Reality-test-Encourage (LIBRE) problem-solving Model application.

Theory provides a framework for what we do and why we make the professional decisions we pursue. This underpinning defines the clinical problem-solving CMA. The importance of theory to practice cannot be overstated. Linking theory to application makes intervention actions understandable and a valuable commodity. Imagine being on a journey without maps or directions; we may never arrive at our desired destination. Theory provides us terrain and weather conditions and as appropriate, detour information that will facilitate our successful arrival. Let's begin: context and social cognitive interactions set the stage for the initial problem-solving work. The problem-solving progress integrates goal orientation, ZPD, and self-regulation. We will therefore begin with theory and then move to the problem-solving application found within the LIBRE Model.

There are several assumptions that accompany the clinical problem-solving model:

1. Mental health services are provided to assist with an identified challenge (often associated with a referral).
2. Every individual has had positive experiences (e.g., values, beliefs, and behaviors) and each has had negative experiences that influenced social cognitive development, a reality that must be acknowledged.
3. The human experience has limits and requires compromises that create gaps (problems) and these gaps (problem areas) introduce learning opportunities.

4. Everyone can learn with scaffold support.
5. Learning to self-regulate is a prerequisite to introducing the skill of attention switching—the shift from one engagement style to another. Attention switching is a learned skill that can be adapted to facilitate social development and social contextual demands. It can also address challenges or gaps.

To facilitate our discussion, each presented theory will be preceded by a subheading. The theory order is structured according to the LIBRE Model problem, solving exchange and will be as follows:

1. Context
2. Social Cognition
3. Goal Orientation
4. Zone of Proximal Development
5. Self-regulation

To illustrate the theory in application, our client's words are used to demonstrate data collected and analyzed. The client's words are the data used to reference the theory. While we will focus on the LIBRE Model problem-solving administration in a later chapter, the goal here is to explore the theoretical framework that supports the model.

Context

The human experience is socially oriented. Bandura describes it as human agency in which we are active participants in our own life stories.[1] We are dynamic members of our daily walk. We live life in community, adaptively changing and developing from there.[2] In some cases, as social learning occurs, there is significant advantage.[3] In other cases, individuals are disadvantaged by the lack of experiences that they have not had to facilitate social skill development.[4] Without argument, we can agree that we have had a combination of advantageous and disadvantageous experiences. Advanced schooling and travel are two examples that contribute to advantaged social development; new awareness is created. Additional nuance socialization considerations are unearthed as perceived advantage or disadvantage experience is introduced. Thus, it may be assumed that increased positive exposure and opportunity provide additional information to better balance the establishment of personal systems.

These early social interactions create trajectories for self-development: constructed social systems that involve other persons. From an early age, we are taught and learn as we interact with caregivers, teachers, mentors, and friends who contribute to our physical and psychosocial needs of survival, safety, social, esteem, and self-actualization.[5] Positive social exchanges facilitate pro-social personal development and an understanding that the client-within-unit is a term used to define a member of a larger contextual, ecological,[6] and bioecological system.[7]

Bronfenbrenner's social-ecological model provides insight to better understand how an individual interacts within a system (e.g., family or community).[8] There are associated arrangements as individuals' function within the context of family. By acknowledging these associations, we are afforded perceptions that would otherwise go unacknowledged. Some of these relationships go beyond the immediate individual to influence and provide critical information about the person. Bronfenbrenner explains that the individual's immediate environment, the microsystem, functions as nested interactions between the individual and the environment. The small child has home and as she grows, new nested systems will include friends and other kin. The term nested is used to illustrate the development of distinct relational memberships that result from extended interactions within distinct contexts.

Reflection

Why it is important for me to know about what my client's family (as a nested system) and what they think, believe and/or value?

This family information allows you the opportunity to begin developing background questions. You will begin to better understand and contextualize your client's needs from the information provided.

The mesosystem describes the connection and interactions between, among, and beyond the microsystems to create the second nested and/or nested within nested structures. Specifically, this may involve the client as a student, learning to negotiate between the family system and other systems. An example is membership within a Boy Scout or Girl Scout troop in which the child will learn new cultural values, mores and socialized behaviors. As the client has experienced life, there may be new or modified systems that are created from those social exchanges.

Beyond the mesosystem is the ecosystem. This system does not directly involve the individual, but does have significant influence upon that person. To illustrate, we present a single mother working several jobs to support her children. The result is that the children spend long periods of time without adult supportive care. The impact on the children has resulted in a lack of emotional security. The time spent alone has created limited social skill development and has introduced insecure behavior around strangers. Thus this ecosystem has impact upon how the child views and interacts with the social environment.

If I want nested within nested client information, what type of question should I ask?

The nested within nested information will address client background information about relationships with distinct communities or influential contexts. First consider what type of system information you seek. For instance, a mesosystem question may explore how your client interacts with a particular teacher within a specific content area or how your client operates with other employees. Or if your client has a best friend, the question may address how they spend their time together. The resulting responses will provide you a better understanding of your client's social connections and experiences outside the home.

An ecosystem question may address how time is spent alone or with others to identify how they have been impacted from the presence or absence of the person. Such as with a child, you may ask, when your mother is not home, what do you do with your time? The reverse would also be useful information. If your mother is home at all times, does her presence make a difference in your activities? Identify the relational impact that may have not been intended, but however did result in a change in your client.

The macrosystem is an umbrella scheme. This system influence affects all of the other systems and accounts for much of the individual's social, cultural, economic, religious, and political views. The significance of the macrosystem is the connecting external factors that influence the client's social development. Understanding the external systems allows for a greater appreciation of why the client thinks and behaves as she does.

Reflection

What are sample questions that could be used to identify macrosystems? Does your family belong to a religious group? What holidays do you celebrate?

Context Application within the LIBRE Model

The LIBRE Model Listen cue sets the stage; the open-ended prompt allows the client to express themselves with added importance to the words, relationships and associated information shared. Bronfenbrenner[9] looks at a person-in-context to examine their social world, conceptualized as a set of concentric circles. Sometimes it is described in terms of the analogy of nested dolls. Our text client, Leah, is a sixteen-year-old pregnant high school student living with her boyfriend, his mother, and his mother's boyfriend. Leah's new microsystem is composed of herself, her boyfriend and their baby. There is however an additional microsystem layer introduced with the boyfriend's mother and his mother's boyfriend. We may likely assume that she is now developmentally moving into a new stage of life and maturity. This assumption may even be supported by her decision to live with her boyfriend. This may or may not be the case. Further, without introducing our cultural values, we listen to hear Leah's story. She reports a change from one family involvement to a new and evolving system. Leah's microsystem (the closest group of people with whom she shares the most in common, which had been her family) has changed. Leah reports that while she is no longer living at home, she remains close to her family of origin. She describes her new family as her boyfriend and new baby. Leah reports that her boyfriend quit school so they could move in together.

Let's pause. As the clinician, it is important to see the detail of what Leah is saying. She is not moving away from her existing connection with the school or even family; rather, she says she wants to finish school and her relations with her family of origin are intact. School and friends remain the same; however, her family is changing. She speaks with neither anger nor sadness as she reports that there is a lot going on. She implies that her parents still love her; the relationship and living conditions, however, have changed.

The second level, the mesosystem, is the larger community with extended family, work, and outside interest groups. Leah's community is expanding. We are introducing new tools of communication as you ask her to identify a primary concern. While we do not have any expressed information about the exosystem (outside influences) or the macrosystem (including laws, cultural systems, and other social mores), we are listening closely to what Leah provides us as contextual information. Our response here may include generating additional questions to addressing potential system influences.

In Bronfenbrenner's early work, he and Morris[10] wrote of an evolving theoretical system for the scientific study of human development over time. They defined bioecological as, "the phenomenon of continuity and change in the biopsychological characteristics of human beings, as individuals and as groups." This theoretical orientation allows for the examination of the person within the environment over time and the examination of the client's interpretation of the environment as interpreted and explained. Thus, the dynamic view of the client as a member of a larger system, or several larger and complex systems, allows for additional inquiry to better assist the client. Culture is one such important consideration. We listen closely to Leah's interpretations of the dynamic system expressions. There are theoretical and intervention implications. For instance, Leah does not see moving in with her boyfriend as outside her norm or expected behavioral mores. Similarly, she does not consider herself a minor. As a clinician, these values and perceptions must be considered with any future intervention.

Social Cognition

Social cognitive experiences involve community. These interactions set the tone for social development. Who and what we attend to speaks volumes to how we see and attend to ourselves. When and where we invest, and to what point we maintain that investment speaks of past experience, skill, and consequence. Bandura[11] explains the human experience as a triadic reciprocal interaction between one's environment, person (values, culture, cognition, beliefs), and behaviors. Thus, as we examine early experiences, this internal interactive dialogue sets the tone for much of one's social development. Equally, culture plays an iatrical part in who we are and how we define self.

Reflection

How do I keep up with this reciprocal interaction?

Active listening is a skill we invest in honing. Listening closely to what the client says will give your insight into the values, beliefs and the client's thoughts as expressed with the words used. Create your strategy and open-ended questions to confirm information received.

Bandura speaks of accomplished interactive determinants. Within counseling, this is suggestive of the many inter-communicative intricacies found within the clients' words and expressions. One example is self-efficacy that involves how we see ourselves in relation to the successful completion of a task. To become self-efficacious clinicians, we must be willing to practice our skills, receive feedback and practice to refine again. As skills develop and positive feedback is received, self-efficacious perceptions result. As clinicians this may include seeing our clients become successful self-regulated persons. For this to occur, we want to take the time to reflect on who and what we are, what we believe along with our own values, so that we do not compromise or hold back in the development of our clinical skills.[12] Our beliefs, values, culture, and investments prepare us to work with clients. We calibrate (adjust our engagement style to maximize our service providing role) to be able to see our clients as distinct persons who each have established communities, skills, and investment patterns (to explore client willingness to consider change). Without regard to individual social cognitive function or dysfunction, each of us deserves dignity and respect.[13] Thus, we must acknowledge the immediate reality that communities vary, as do individuals. This variability defines the distinct role of the client within community from that of the service provider, that is, the clinician. Smith and Montilla[14] explain that culture has been found to hold back or compromise clinician skill development. Self-regulated and invested service providers actively process their thoughts, feelings, culture and attitudes. Clinician success is linked to personal investment and the commitment skill development and self-awareness of weaknesses and with a plan to address those areas. Efficacy is associated with perception which in turn influences motivation and persistence. According to Bandura, self-efficacy addresses our specific beliefs about their capabilities.

Reflection

OK, I need to develop my own self-efficacy; I get that, but what about the client?

How do I present self-efficacy to a client? Self-efficacy is developed over time. As you model problem-solving self-efficacy, you are teaching problem-solving. As your working relationship develops, you will be able to provide feedback so the clients will begin to identify their own self-efficacy.

The importance of the social cognitive theory[15] is in the reciprocal relation of behavior, environment, and person. Each of these interacts to determine or influence one's individuality and behavior. Bandura defines the nature of the individual as a combination of number of basic capabilities. For example, personality and values interact to influence behavior even as behavior influences values and environment, which also influence and interact with and are influenced by the environment. These three dimensions interact with each other to produce the person's social cognitive contextual views, which the individual sees, holds as a capacity, believes, and is prepared to act upon. Contextual environments are at times taken for granted, but environmental interactions contribute to who we are and what we believe. Our values and our interactions are affected with other people's influences.

Reflection

This sounds simple and complex at the same time. How do I ask questions about my client's environment, behavior and personal beliefs and values while self-regulating my own views so they don't influence what I hear my client saying. How do I do that?

This is definitely a complex interaction; however, the problem-solving activity will facilitate with your environment, behavior, and person questions. Also remember to develop questions ahead of time to facilitate asking social cognitive questions. It will always be important for you to self-regulate.

Social cognition application within the LIBRE Model. Three LIBRE Model prompts address social cognitive information: Listen, Brainstorm, and Reality-test. Leah's LMSF responses indicate that she lives at home, attends school and is doing well academically. Environmentally she indicates that she is the first in her family to attend high school. Also of interest is the self-efficacy suggested in her willingness to address and solve an identified problem: living conditions. She holds the perception of possibility, suggesting that she may change. We see Leah's person as she prepares to explore her brainstormed options and workable reality-testing (behavior) as she explores what that will look like if she acts upon the option. Leah extends her boundaries of possibilities with suggestions:

1. I could tell my boyfriend's mother to leave.
2. I could tell her boyfriend to leave.
3. I could leave.
4. I could do nothing.
5. I could talk to my boyfriend about how we need to talk with his mother and her boyfriend.

Leah offers key information about her values, culture, past experiences with adults and even about how she processes a challenge. Leah's behavioral responses are important. While any of the options may have worked, what is significant is the elimination of options. She deleted options 1–4, and the one option that she selected to keep, option 5, was to talk with her boyfriend. The reality-testing is that behavioral representation. She began to process the action involved and what that would look like as she sequenced her steps. We now have a picture of Leah's social cognitive processing. She has given us a model of how she will proceed with this challenge. This representation, however, does not suggest more than a willingness to process her concern. To be able to see commitment, we would need to see her willingness to both identify a specific goal within her control and then follow through to create a workable plan with timelines that would suggest a further level of accountability.

Reflection

What evidence do I have that will help me to know if the clients are committed to the goals they set?

To be able to see commitment, we would need to see the willingness to both identify a goal with some specificity and create a workable plan with timelines.

Goal Orientation

Much has been written about goal orientation and goal investment: Schunk and Ertmer[16] and Zimmerman[17] explain its importance in creating, facilitating, and supporting change. Goal orientation is considered a motivational or movement investment. The focus is on the goal and the possibility for positive change. Goal orientation is the individual's engagement in achieving a focal activity[18] and may be thought of as the reason for the investment.[19] Drawing from learning theory, a performance goal is composed of one focused point of attention, initial task investment and the perseverance to invest in the task up to completion. Self-efficacy (how you see yourself in relation to the identified task and skill in accomplishing that task) facilitates not only investment, but also whether there is no task completion investment. If the individual believes the goal is obtainable, there is an increased focus on that goal acquisition. There is a greater self-regulated effort in pursuit of the goal. Examining the client's efficacy is important. If the individual believes the goal is obtainable, there is an increased likelihood of self-regulated effort expended toward pursuit of that goal.[20]

Reflection

When I listen to my clients, should I be listening to how they define themselves? What am I looking for in their goal definition?

As your clients define goals for themselves, listen to the words they use and how they describe themselves. Listen to hear if they define themselves as passive or active; listen for specificity and detail in the questions they provide. Ask if they have a history of accomplishing the goals they set. You are listening for prior experience in goal setting and accomplishment of those goals.

Goal Orientation application within the LIBRE Model. The two LIBRE Model prompts that elicit goal orientation are Identify a Concern and Encourage. As we examine the data Leah provided, we see a self-defined goal: What can I do to support my boyfriend? As we examine the steps to her best solution, we see specificity suggesting both self-efficacy and self-regulated behavior:

1. I need to ask my boyfriend to meet me at the grocery store so we can talk.
2. Then we can decide what we are going to tell his mother and her boyfriend.
3. We will need to decide what we are going to do if they don't pay anything.

Leah's processing is linear, logical, and clearly articulated. The accountability for her plan is shown by her willingness to create a timeline, which she does without hesitation. Leah plans to ask her boyfriend to meet her at the grocery store today for them to decide what they are going to tell his mother and her boyfriend. By next month, she explains that they will know what to do and she gives herself two months to decide with her boyfriend their next steps. She solidifies her commitment with her personalized mantra: We can do this! We have options to move forward!

Zone of Proximal Development

The ZPD provides a supportive path for change.[21] Described as a socially mediated process, the ZPD asserts that learning is structured activity involving supportive language interactions. The assumption is that if you scaffold the task, the individual will learn. Vygotsky conceptualized this as supportive learning and explained that young children use self-talk and social exchanges to practice and learn. The notion is that each person has a zone of development; however, to maximize learning, supportive assistance must be provided. You will need to identify at what point the skill ends so that the learning may be taught and practiced. This is the moment when supportive scaffold is provided to learn the new task.

ZPD application within LIBRE Model. The LMSFT becomes the mediated assistance through extended learning resulting in social development. The prompts of the LIBRE Model provide the supportive guidance for problem-solving. The LMSFT facilitates the client's application of social cognitive thoughts and goal orientation.

Reflection

Scaffolding sounds good but it also sounds like it will require an additional investment from me; how do I do that? What are the implications or consequences?

An example may help; you will be listening for gaps in the clients' thinking. Once you confirm that what you heard is correct, you will want to begin addressing those gaps to teach your clients new skills. For example, your client has been in many fights. You ask how he knows he needs to fight. He replies that it is the way the person looks at him. You confirm. If someone looks at you a particular way, you will fight him? He says, yes. You then use open-ended questions that may include: What if the person is not really looking at you? What if he just forgot to wear his glasses that day? Would that make a difference in your thoughts to fight him? Now you are ready to scaffold the new behavior as an intervention. You now can teach your client to test that what he thinks he is seeing before he acts on what he thought he saw.

How the client frames the problem provides information about prior learned and experienced responses. The resolutions they create suggest how they have sustained investment toward meeting a goal or defined challenge. Meaningfulness comes from the responses to the prompts. As with the ZPD, the ultimate goal is that the client will be able to both enter into the problem-solving exchange and remain invested through to the development of a workable resolution. The focus is learning how to solve problems and how to accommodate environmental and intrapersonal challenges. Initial and sustained attention found within the LIBRE Model activity responses demonstrates how the proximal zone of development is scaffolded by the supportive prompts.

Self-Regulation

Zimmerman[22] explains self-regulation as having both cognitive and affective components. It involves self-management. As we prepare to work with our clients, we want to be able to see their views. Self-regulation is found in my managed responsible role as a service provider and not to insert myself within the LIBRE Model responses. In application, I may have opinions and the perfect advice to offer; however, no matter how enticing the scenario is or how it draws me in, my role and responsibility is to listen. Listening and providing the prompts are my service. I focus on my client and away from my opinions. While I am free to clarify prompts and offer examples as requested, my primary attention is to verbal and nonverbal client expressions. I intentionally model self-regulation for my clients, remembering to be mindful of the complexity of the human experience. I am attentive to the social cognitive cues that are being shared even within the simplest communication. The entire LIBRE Model exchange has multicognitive elements, from identifying a problem to brainstorming to reality-testing. As the client becomes skilled in self-management and problem-solving, the problem-solving and engagement styles can be adjusted through regulated attention switching. A skilled self-managed clinician will self-adjust to accommodate the client's needs.

Reflection

Self-regulation begins with my not introducing personal biases. How then do I introduce my client to his/her self-regulation?

Beyond modeling, you will want to record your clients' words and actions so you have data. As the working relationship continues, then you are able to present this collected data. This will allow you to assist your client in making connections because you will be sharing patterns of behavior with their own words; it will be easier for them to see the direct application. They will be able to see their self-regulated behavior over time as recorded from the data. This introduces the opportunity to teach from a strength-based perspective; you are collecting their successes as well as their non–self-regulated behaviors and the consequences of those actions.

Summary

The theoretical underpinning of the clinical problem-solving approach incorporates theory in application to allow us to see client learning and social cognitive development. Our discussion thus far has included context, social cognitive, goal orientation, ZPD, and self-regulation theories as displayed in client's problem-solving words and expressions. These exchanges set the stage for meaningful counseling. Socratic questions provide the open-ended discussion to better facilitate our client's mental health development as well as, to re-state key thoughts.

Who the client is and what the client shares verbally and nonverbally through behaviors will offer volumes of information. Client words are recorded verbatim and nonverbal expressions are noted as observations in self-development, self-efficacy and problem-solving. This data can then be used to better assist the client. Social cognitive theory, goals and goal setting are fundamental tenets of motivation. Bandura[23] asserts that motivation is goal-directed described as intentionality. Within the problem-solving activity, it is demonstrated as initiated and sustained attention by the individual's expectations, behavior, and self-efficacy—again referencing the interactions that person, behavior, and environment have in relation to each other.

The problem-solving activity involves theories as processes toward workable gains or outcomes. If the client is limited within the problem-solving responses, further background questions may be required. You may select to stop the activity. For example, if the client is only able to offer information from the Listen prompt, she may not know how to self-regulate to address a challenge. She may not see herself in a position of effecting change. By stopping to ask additional questions about the affect and client's prior experiences, you will be able to collect additional information about why the client is stumped. Once the need is confirmed, a case plan may be developed. In Leah's case, it will be important to see if she is able to and/or does complete her identified plan. If she has had some success with her resolution plan, you may want her to complete the LIBRE Model problem-solving activity again.

Practice Client Exercise

Jon has been living out of his car and going to the community shelter each morning before work to wash and prepare himself for the day. He has been referred to you because his boss has just discovered this behavior. What social cognitive and goal-oriented questions will you ask Jon, and what type of information would you anticipate being provided?

NOTES

1. Albert Bandura, "Toward a Psychology of Human Agency," *Perspectives on Psychological Science* 1, no. 2 (2006): 164–180.

2. Albert Bandura, *Social Foundations of Thought and Action: A Social Cognitive Theory* (Upper Saddle River, NJ: Pearson Education Prentice Hall, 1986).

3. Neal Krause, "Longitudinal Study of Social Support and Meaning in Life," *Psychology and Aging* 22, no. 3 (2007): 456–469.

4. Kipling D. Williams, "Ostracism," *Annual Review of Psychology* 58, (2007): 425–452.

5. Abraham H. Maslow, *Toward a Psychology of Being*, 2nd ed. (New York: D. Van Nostrand, 1968).

6. Urie Bronfenbrenner, "Ecology of the Family as a Context for Human Development: Research Perspectives," *Developmental Psychology* 22, no. 6 (1986): 723–742.

7. Urie Bronfenbrenner and Pamela A. Morris, "The Bioecological Model of Human Development," in *Handbook of Child Psychology*, 6th ed., edited by William Damon and Richard M. Lerner (Hoboken, NJ: John Wiley & Sons, 2006), 793–828.

8. Urie Bronfenbrenner, *The Ecology of Human Development: Experiments by Nature and Design* (Cambridge, MA: Harvard University Press, 1979).

9. Urie Bronfenbrenner, *The Ecology of Human Development: Experiments by Nature and Design* (Cambridge, MA: Harvard University Press, 1979); Urie Bronfenbrenner, "Ecology of the Family as a Context for Human Development: Research Perspectives," *Developmental Psychology* 22, no. 6 (1986): 723–742.

10. Urie Bronfenbrenner and Pamela A. Morris, "The Bioecological Model of Human Development," in *Handbook of Child Psychology*, 6th ed., edited by William Damon and Richard M. Lerner (Hoboken, NJ: John Wiley & Sons, 2006), 793.

11. Albert Bandura, "Social Cognitive Theory: An Agentic Perspective," *Annual Review of Psychology* 52 (2001): 1–26.

12. Norma S. Guerra, "LIBRE Model: Engagement Styles in Counseling." *Journal of Employment Counseling*, 44 (2007): 2–10.

13. Patricia Arredondo, "Multicultural Competencies and Family Therapy Strategies with Latino Families," in *Counseling and Family Therapy with Latino Populations*, edited by Robert L. Smith and R. Esteban Montilla (New York: Routledge Taylor & Francis Group, 2006), 77–95.

14. Robert L. Smith and R. Esteban Montilla. *Counseling and Family Therapy with Latino Populations* (New York: Routledge Taylor & Francis Group, 2006).

15. Albert Bandura, *Social Foundations of Thought and Action: A Social Cognitive Theory* (Upper Saddle River, NJ: Pearson Education Prentice Hall, 1986).

16. Dale H. Schunk and Peggy A. Ertmer, "Self-Regulation and Academic Learning: Self-Efficacy Enhancing Interventions," in *Handbook of Self-Regulation*, edited by Monique Boekaerts, Paul R. Pintrich and Moshe Zeidner (San Diego: American Press, 2000), 631–649.

17. Berry J. Zimmerman, "The Development of Scientific Reasoning Skills," *Development Review 20 (2000):* 99–149.

18. Dale H. Schunk, *Learning Theories: An Educational Perspective* (Boston, MA: Allyn & Bacon, 2012).

19. Eric M. Anderman, Chammie C. Austin and Dawn M. Johnson, "The Development of Goal Orientation," in *Development of Achievement Motivation*, edited

by Allan Wigfield and Jacquelynne S. Eccles (San Diego: Academic Press, 2002), 197–220.

20. Andrew J. Elliot and Holly A. McGregor, "A 2 × 2 Achievement Goal Framework," *Journal of Personality and Social Psychology* 80, no. 3 (2001): 501–519.

21. Lev S. Vygotsky, *Mind in Society: The Development of Higher Psychological Processes* (Cambridge, MA: Harvard University Press, 1978).

22. Berry J. Zimmerman, "The Development of Scientific Reasoning Skills." *Development Review* 20 (2000): 99–149.

23. Albert Bandura, *Self-Efficacy: The Exercise of Control* (New York: Freeman, 1997).

Chapter 3

The Clinician

Service Provider

At the core of professional growth and development is a self-regulated commitment to specific goals and the monitoring of ongoing skill development.

Objective: To assess the service provider's role and commitment to self as a pre-requisite component of counseling.

Professional development is an investment made both before and during one's career. It involves learning and refining specialized skills consistent with identified ethical standards. Technical language may vary from one mental health specialization to the next; however, all share common principles, values, and mores. For example, the clinician (a term used throughout this text interchangeably with service provider) has the goal of providing the best effective service to assist individuals in need. This is completed without causing harm while maintaining skills and sensitivity to cultural and ethnic diversity and to the advancement of the profession.[1] There is no short-changing this commitment. Attaining professional identity is naturally linked to attentive engagement and personal self-management, that is, self-regulation within the helping role. These foundational requisites are important to all healthy service provider practices and, by extension, to strong mental wellness.

This chapter encourages you to consider positive and effective professional engagement styles that are characteristic of and contribute to positive identity development and away from potential harm. Attaining professional skills and identity are foundational in developing and maintaining a skilled practice. This self-regulated awareness may be accomplished using the LIBRE Model problem-solving activity.

Identity development suggests change. Positive social cognitive changes or adjustments are components of client transformation; accordingly, it would seem appropriate that we as service providers pursue change with this same positive zest. Our motivation is to be the most effective professionals possible. Bandura[2] frames change in terms of self-processing that is orchestrated through meaningful social-situational feedback. Opportunities for self-development occur as a result of positive social cognitive feedback. Therefore, whether you are a novice or experienced service provider, it is important to devise a PDP designed to improve skills with external self-checks to monitor progress. Professional and personal wellness is important when assisting others, with personal wellness as the foundation. Here is a somber example: If I am drowning, I will not be able to save the life of someone else, not to mention myself—this is not where we want to find ourselves. We want to be the skilled lifeguard who throws out the lifesaver to bring the drowning person to safety. The more skilled we are (e.g., actively listening and attending to verbal and nonverbal cues), the more successful we will become in facilitating client change and managing our professional selves.

Understanding Engagement Styles

Let's begin by defining engagement styles as a behavioral manifestation of initial and sustained attentiveness.[3] Engagement is active, goal-directed, flexible, constructive, persistent, and/or may include focused attention.[4] Here we introduce four observable engagement variants, including unfiltered highly motivated attentiveness, filtered attentiveness, a limited initial attentiveness, and a modified attentiveness once a goal investment is determined.[5] There are positive and negative aspects to each engagement style; however, for the clinician, the importance is found balancing the client's engagement with one's own. You must know your preferred engagement style and manage it as a tool in working with your client. For example, if you maintain an actual (unfiltered highly motivated attentiveness) engagement style to address the client need, you are more in the mindset to make sure to provide your client the space to express his own engagement style. This then becomes your starting place and sets up opportunities to introduce new or modified engagement styles that may better serve the client's needs. Thus, what you are doing is calibrating your engagement to best meet the needs of your client.

Reflection

When I calibrate my engagement style, will it be to match the client or the client need?

You may want to match your client's engagement style to better establish rapport; however, you will likely need to cognitively switch to an engagement style that will facilitate his willingness to explore change.

Avoid a mismatch of engagement styles. For instance, if your client has a venting engagement style, identifying this style of engagement will allow you the opportunity to teach him how to extend his attention further to learn how to develop goals and change rather than remaining in a ruminating role. If you are more goal-focused in your engagement, you could likely find yourself frustrated because your client never moves beyond venting. Your frustration now becomes the focus of the exchange. Rather than investing in an intervention to teach your client how to set goals, you may decide that this client really has no desire to change, thereby losing a moment to create change.

Chapter 7 contains further information about engagement styles. For now, let's examine four engagement styles and what they look like as professional postures using the following four hand positions to illustrate.

Actual Engagement

The open palm provides an illustration of a constructive, unfiltered, encouraging, and self-aware service provider (see Figure 3.1). This attentive engagement is open, committed to new knowledge and environmental skill experiences from the beginning to the conclusion of the therapeutic session. The service provider is clearly attentive to the client's needs and is able to distinguish personal or professional clinician needs from those of the client. The service provider knows and understands culture as a personal life experience; thereby viewing and respecting the client according to verbally expressed and nonverbally shared cultural mores. The clinician listens,

Figure 3.1 Open Palm Hand Position Illustration of Actual Engagement

records notes and anticipates where the client is headed. The service provider maintains professional awareness to be open to client information provided. Once outside the session, if there is additional research to be acquired, the professional commitment is there to learn about the client's background.

Reflection

Can anyone be an actual engaged person? If I don't know how, how do I become actual engaged?

Without realizing it, we spend a sizable amount of time as actual engaged. One example is driving your car to an unfamiliar location. You are attentive to what is happening as you drive until you reach your destination. You are an actual engaged person. If not actually engaged, you will likely not arrive at your desired destination. The actual engagement is developed with reflection, examples, and increased awareness. The LIBRE Model problem-solving activity will provide you an opportunity to monitor and increase your self-awareness.

Actual engagement Professional Development Plan (PDP) characteristics. The service provider's ongoing PDP is managed from a strength-based perspective in which new skills, experiences, and individualized learning goals with timelines and benchmarks are identified. There is a built-in commitment to identify new professional proficiencies. In terms of engagement styles, this is referred to as an actual engagement, with a strong initial and sustained investment and is most recognizable as classic engagement behavior.[6] The individual is reflective, open, and willing to explore, learn, and synthesize.

Potential Engagement

The opposite of actual engagement is potential engagement, characterized by the clenched fist (see Figure 3.2). The service provider adopts filtering behaviors to foster control, minimize professional risk, and limit client investment. This closed posture occurs from the beginning, as the client enters the room, through to the close of the session. Without much attention to self-regulated boundaries, this engagement style has built-in screening checkpoints so distance is maintained and no real attentiveness or investment occurs. Behaviorally, the service provider may hold a closed position within the counseling session with either legs or arms crossed—or both. This service provider may select to be verbally expressive by barraging clients with closed-ended questions. The client often feels of less value, sometimes intimidated by the exchange. The message this service provider presents is keep your distance and I will keep mine. This engagement style introduces

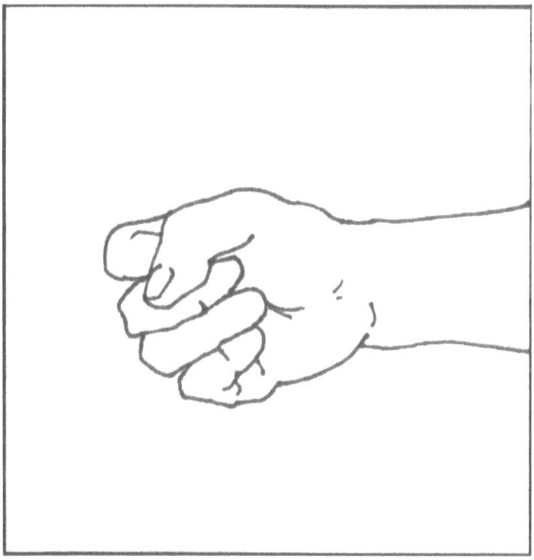

Figure 3.2 Clenched Fist Hand Position Illustration of Potential Engagement

problematic limitations. For example, one unanticipated side effect is the comfortable position of becoming a power-laden, controlling clinician. The service provider defines the counseling session according to personal style, never allowing the client to address any significant need in a way comfortable to her. Service providers with this engagement style are likely to prefer clients with the same filtered approach; their goal is to keep all interactions general and nonspecific. One notable advantage of this style is that the clinician is likely never to become overextended or too close to any client.

Reflection

Is it bad to have a potential engagement style?

There are positive and negative aspects to each engagement style. If you have a client who is overly aggressive and wanting to extend beyond all appropriate boundaries, then this engagement style might be appropriate to establish necessary boundaries.

Potential engagement PDP characteristics. Assuming this engagement approach will likely limit your professional development. The clinician's PDP is broad and undefined with no specific goals or timelines; ongoing learning is not a priority. There is a general tone that learning comes with time and experience. Any significant learning comes from guided or directed instruction as opposed to self-managed investment.

Venting Engagement

The hyper-immediacy of this engagement style is illustrated with the wringing of hands (see Figure 3.3). This service provider becomes so invested in client needs that boundaries are blurred, resulting in compromised client service. The service provider is open to the immediacy of the client's needs with a tendency to rush in and rescue, rather than to explore the opportunity to provide an intervention, which may result in acquisition of a new skill. Within a session, these service providers are most skilled in identifying and understanding clients' environment and social cognitive needs. The clinician's risk is unknowingly stepping into an enabler role (a position that will assist in reinforcing the clients' maladaptive behaviors), thus encouraging client dependence. For this service provider, the initial engagement is lively; however, rather than moving forward to the planning of goals, the service provider deliberately remains in the defining of the problem stage, concluding each session without moving beyond problem identification. In terms of engagement styles, venting engagement can be characterized by storytelling. The service provider both likes a good story and tells a good story. No significant self-reflection occurs; the clinician never considers that this behavior could be a contributing factor to the clients' needs or problems. By the end of the day, this service provider is exhausted from defining clients' stories and working as an enabler so that clients remain in the midst of identified concerns. The focus of this clinician's engagement is on the story, not resolutions or growth. The clinician's affect

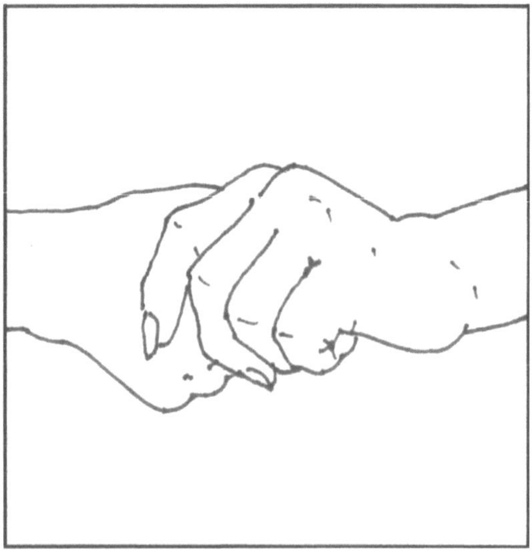

Figure 3.3 Wringing Hand Position Illustration of Venting Engagement

may likely be clouded by a "they really need me" attitude. Codependency is a likely product of this hand-wringing venting engagement style.

Reflection

If I like to vent and that initial attention in first listening to the client, how do I make sure that I don't become overly invested in the client's story?

Self-regulation and knowing yourself will be your best management plan. Develop a strategy with cues that will preclude your becoming overly invested in the client's story.

Venting engagement PDP characteristics. Assuming this engagement approach, there is likelihood that the service provider will not sustain the necessary attention to accomplish identified plans. This service provider prefers to initiate PDP with great detail in all the skills they would like to learn; however, their plan will lack specific timelines or steps toward completion. As a colleague once explained: I am great at initiating change. Is it really that important that I follow-through? Isn't initiating enough?

Goal-Focused Engagement

The fourth hand position is the cupped hand (see Figure 3.4). This clinician operates from a well self-defined role. This goal-focused style is directed to

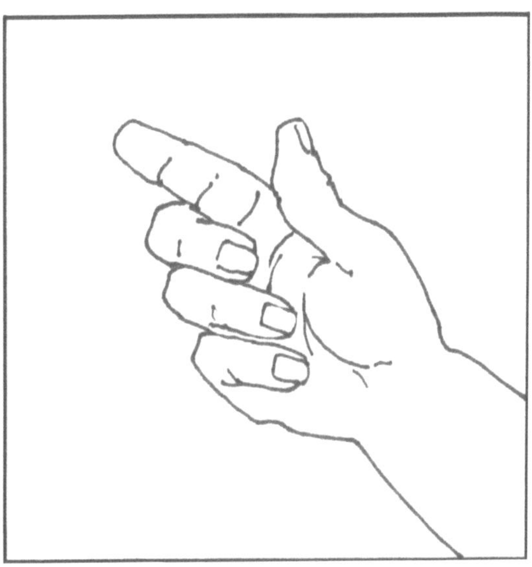

Figure 3.4 Cupped Hand Position Illustration of Goal-focused Engagement

problem resolution from the initial contact through to the close of the session. The service provider is attentive to the goal, which provides direction to the session. These service providers are deliberate in their intent to provide defined services. This clinician identifies goals, develops detailed plans and follows up to complete them. While this sounds like the ideal posture for a service provider, as mentioned earlier, there are positive and negative aspects to each engagement style. For the goal-focused engagement style, you will want to make sure that your goals do not become more important than your clients' goals.

Reflection

What can I do to make sure that my goal does not become more important than my client's goal?

Self-awareness is critical, calibrating to an actual engagement style will assist focusing on your client's goal.

Goal-focused engagement style PDP characteristics. This professional development perspective is linked to counseling skills that have had positive returns with current clients and a focused desire on helping future clients. This style is likely to have a built-in personal commitment to become better: to identify needed new skills, to develop those skills, to evaluate the acquired learning, and to apply the newly developed skills. Hence, goal-focused clinicians' professional development plans will likely be personalized with detailed monitoring benchmarks to gauge skill development and care for self.

Becoming a Learned, Skilled Clinician

At the core of professional growth and development is a self-regulated commitment to specific goals and the monitoring of ongoing skill development. Professional development needs are organized by personal and professional defined strengths and weaknesses. They are self-regulated (with time and skill development) and monitored for quality through mentoring and other means of benchmarking gains. Of the above four engagement styles, the actual and goal-focused engagement styles provide the greater advantage. With these, active sustained change is maintained. The potential and venting engagement styles do not have the sustained attentiveness to seek or achieve change. Thus, monitoring yourself and your interactions when working with a client becomes an important responsibility toward introducing change.

Reflection

Why are actual and goal-focused engagement styles better?

There is a sustained attentiveness in both of these engagement styles that will introduce the opportunity for active client change.

Without regard to the engagement style you select, developing a risk-management contingency to monitor your investment in session and in practice is important to your overall professional development and accountability. This risk management plan will address what I will do when faced with a crisis, potential crisis, or anticipated challenge. The risk plan can address small risks. For example, if I have a preference to vent, how do I keep my venting out of the counseling session? Or it may be a larger risk. For example, I determine that it is too large a risk to see clients in the building on the weekend when no one else is around. Thus, my risk management plans will state that I will only see clients during the assigned workday. While not all service providers or mental health professions are the same; they do share the integrity, ethical care for others, and self-care as foundations. What you do to personalize, protect, and grow becomes your commitment to professional identity development with your assessed strengths and weaknesses in mind.

Outline of PDP with Risk Management Contingencies

I. Identify specific professional development annual goal(s)
   a. Describe each goal in detail with the required skill to be learned
   b. Describe how you will measure and monitor the newly acquired skill(s)

II. Develop identified strengths
   a. Identify strengths
   b. Develop a plan to refine or enhance the identified strengths
   c. Develop an implementation plan—conditions under which the strength will be used
   d. Develop an accountability plan—monitoring and benchmarking of that skill

III. Develop identified weaknesses
   a. Identify each weakness
   b. Develop a plan to refine identified weakness
   c. Develop an implementation plan—conditions under which you may be called upon to use this weakness
   d. Develop an accountability plan—monitoring and benchmarking of the developed skill to compensate for the identified weakness

IV. Create a self-regulation plan
   a. Create a self-care plan
   b. Develop a plan to monitor your self-care

V. Monitor engagement style use
   a. Develop a system to calibrate engagement for each client
   b. Identify how you will manage your preferred engagement style
VI. Design a risk management contingency
   a. Develop a plan that outlines the parameters of client mental health services
   b. Identify potential crises and how each will be managed
   c. Identify the criteria that introduces risk
   d. Develop a plan to handle an unanticipated risk
VII. Identify an annual closure to the targeted professional development goals
   a. Develop a calendar schedule with specific dates to review the PDP
   b. Develop a listing of encouraging words and expressions that inspire

Clinician Adaptability

Identity development does not follow a universal path; therefore, develop your path to allow your strengths to guide your skill and services. Bandura[7] proposes four core emergent properties that make up individual development:

Intentionality: formation of plans and strategy development

Forethought: goals and projected outcomes that guide and motivate intentionality

Self-reactiveness: selection of appropriate self-regulated choices and actions for the completion of identified plans

Self-reflectiveness: metacognitive process involving self-examination of personal thoughts and efficiency

These concepts are especially pertinent for us as clinicians providing mental health services to individuals-in-need. I must be able to develop my PDP to be able to move forward with the specific strategy to guide me toward meaningful learning. Self-reflection becomes my safeguard to remaining committed to my craft and self-development to my skill enhancement.

Mental wellness is an essential clinician investment. While this is by no means an exhaustive listing, presented here are questions to encourage you to develop yourself as a skilled service provider. As a clinician, you must continue to visit and revisit your personalized levels of self-regulated intentionality.

Reflection

What purposeful plans and strategy must I develop to reach a maximized skill level that will facilitate successful client gains?

- What investment must I make to maintain or acquire skill proficiency?
- What must I do to create those opportunities to learn?
- What types of support do I need to be effective?
- What are my checks and balances to efficiency and effectiveness as a counselor?

The answers are for you to ponder and for you to provide. My commitment to forethought is managed by my goals and projected outcomes, which guide and motivate my client and myself.

- What are my goals?
- Are they specific?
- Does the level of specificity allow for discernible outcome measurement?
- Do my goals motivate me?
- Do I have internal and external checkpoints to hold myself accountable?
- Do I make provision for celebration each time a client or I accomplish a goal?
- When I fall short, do I have a strategy to redirect myself?

These are your questions to ponder and yours to respond.

For my self-reactiveness, I must manage my self-regulated choices and actions simultaneously as the means of processing my self-identified PDP and my counseling services. Therefore, I must be ready to revisit my choices and actions if they are not resulting in my professional best.

Formative (ongoing) and summative (culminating) self-assessments are important to be able to make appropriate adjustments. Accordingly, as I pursue my goals, I must build upon subgoals with benchmarked feedback as indicators to make sure that I remain on track. For example, while formative feedback may look or feel arduous (why do I have to research working with at-risk families before seeing them as clients), this feedback may actually assist me in redirecting myself. Perhaps after reading about this population, I realize that I really don't want to work with this group. It is important to frame learning as positive and constructive.

Here are questions to get you started

- How do I use the feedback I receive to accomplish my goals?
- How do I let go of those choices and actions that don't facilitate the execution of my immediate and/or overall goals?
- Within my place of self-reflectiveness, I must encourage myself to examine my personal thoughts and efficiency and effectiveness.
- Am I caring for myself so I may care for others?

- Am I receiving and recognizing internal (self-talk) and external (what others tell me or show me with their behaviors) feedback to meet my professional goals?
- When I fail, do I have the resiliency and protective factors (supportive friends, family, or others) to stand up and go forward?
- Are my personal thoughts helping me?
- Having established a PDP, we are ready to begin working with the problem-solving CMA. The following series of questions will facilitate our conversation about this clinical problem-solving CMA.
- What is the clinical problem-solving CMA?

The problem-solving CMA is the organizing structure to the counseling exchange. What is the LIBRE Model? The LIBRE Model is a problem-solving activity that includes the following prompts:

- Listen and list key information (for example, referral information)
- Identify the focus
- Brainstorm possible options
- Reality-test (the maintained items are developed to explore what it would look like if they were acted upon) or pursued
- Encourage involves the development of a plan with timelines

How does the clinical problem-solving CMA assist me in preparing for a session? The clinician is primarily responsible for developing and implementing direct client services. Thus, internal and external preparation for services begins with the clinician. Using the CMA, it may look like this:

- Listening to yourself. How comfortable are you with this referral/problem? Do you have experience with working with someone from this background?
- Identify your goal. For instance, it might be how you will address your client's first meeting.
- Brainstorm. Consider options to accomplish your identified goal.
- Reality-test. This may involve a more realistic examination of your options.
- Encourage. This final step allows for the development of a plan with timelines. Your plan may be to provide the client a culturally competent initial intake by asking nonjudgmental neutral, open-ended questions.

While cultural competency is not achieved solely by being a skilled active listener, such a listener is better prepared to recognize presented cultural information. Be ready to learn as you listen. Age, ethnicity, culture, disability, gender, religion, sexual orientation, marital status, and socioeconomic status are social cognitive cultural indicators. This will require that you learn and ask the client about cultural mores, values, and beliefs so you do not inadvertently offend.

Ask questions to confirm your understanding. You will find that parallel to the PDP you created for yourself, you may develop a plan for how best to understand and address client's identified needs. This information is added to your client's CMP. Any external readings or research on the client's culture may also be added and used as a reference. The more you learn of the client's culture, the better you will be able to assist the client.

Remember that monitoring client boundaries is an ongoing investment. Never overextend yourself in time or energy when working with a client. For example, consider a client that you really enjoy working with. You want to learn about your client's culture and you have received an invitation to a family cultural celebration. You think, this is great, and you really want to go. You see yourself working with this culture in the future; this is a great opportunity. This may easily become a slippery situation. Your self-reflected awareness is your safeguard. You realize that you may confuse your client by assuming more than one role. You also quickly realize that you have moved away from the client's needs to begin thinking about your personal needs. You problem solve and decide that introducing this additional relationship may complicate your service provider role; you are not the client's friend. Your problem resolution is to thank your client for the invitation but not attend, hereby holding to your professional role as a clinician.

Reflection

What is the problem-solving Case Management Portfolio (CMP)?

The CMP is the case folder where all client information is maintained. Counseling has many points of contact and critical client information. These documents should be kept together. Tables may be developed to better track client change, and these data points should be visited and revisited often. The help provider should feel free to share the collected information with the client to celebrate client gains. As you close the CMA services, you will use the CMP information to develop the client resiliency plan. Contextualizing client gains and challenges that have been overcome will assist with the development of strategies as the client moves away from counseling. The client should be given the opportunity to keep copies of all LIBRE Model problem-solving exchanges and if they want copies of the tables that have tracked their patterns, which too should be offered.

What documents are kept in the CMP?

This portfolio is a central repository for problem-solving activity(s), social cognitive and goal-setting experiences, background information, and intervention data.

What does the problem-solving Case Management Approach (CMA) look like when used in consultation?

The CMA, discussed in greater detail in a later chapter is introduced here in response to this question. The CMA used for indirect or consultative services will involve working with someone who is providing the direct counseling services. When in this role, you will want to monitor the engagement style of your consultee as well as the reported engagement style of the client. Established parameters within the consultative role set the stage for the communication. These parameters include: (1) Who is requesting your assistance; (2) What does the service provider have as expectations; and (3) Are there any other expectations that need to be defined or clarified with the referral? In one sense, the service provider becomes your client and the client is the concern. Self-regulated monitoring is as important with consultation as it is in counseling; you do not want to overextend your role. For example, assuming that the service provider needs and wants help, he asks you to come and see his client. Is this appropriate? No. Instead, in your self-regulated and monitoring role you might suggest that you role-play until he feels comfortable to go back to see his client. The consultant works within the established referral to consult, teach, or assist. Role boundaries are maintained, working with the service provider to focus on the counselor's strengths, offering new or modified skills to address cultural and social cognitive needs. The client receives direct services from the clinician (who is receiving consultation) without ever meeting the consultant.

What does a fine-tuned service approach look like?

Skilled clinicians, like surgeons, make precise psychological cuts that are open-ended questions, working closely with clients to examine thoughts, feelings, and behaviors. Troublesome thoughts, feelings and consequences are examined to construct or reconstruct new pathways of thought. This can be quite a complex task so begin with client-defined social context, and then add from there. Use her thoughts and feelings as gauges to identify any maladaptive thinking that could result in maladaptive behavior. As you reflect on your professional strengths, remember that clients too have personal strengths that are assets to be incorporated and utilized. Teach your clients to be independent and skilled problem solvers. Monitoring the client's openness to change will facilitate learning and the sustainability of new skills. Thus, professional self-awareness, the ongoing commitment to skill development and established wellness self-checks are important for both the client and the clinician.

You are a problem-solving clinician who introduces opportunity for reflective behavioral and cognitive expression. The problem-solving steps used to manage professional development are the same steps that you will use in your practice with clients. You are committed to resolution, client growth, and client skill development even as you pursue your best professional self. Similarly, you want your clients to develop into the best that they can be. Congruency (being genuine, trustworthy and agreeable in how you present yourself) and self-congruency (being true to yourself) are important values to and for the clinician; they also describe how best to approach and process change.

We work within social cognitive contexts moving across different groups, cultures, and systems. How do we ensure we maintain our effectiveness? A good analogy is a pilot moving from one destination to the next. The path is never straight. We consider weather and atmospheric pressure changes along with other traffic and changing variables. The same holds true in counseling. While working with the client, you may discover social, cultural, and cognitive challenges. We have skill but we never have the same experiences as our clients. It is important to attend to stated and unstated messages in order to move away from the risk of responding to a client from our general or personal experiences rather than from the trained counseling perspective.

The pilot deliberately moves to accommodate air turbulence and avoid other air traffic. Patience, active listening, and a carefully sustained engagement are important. Reflect. A well-defined ethical position will involve seeking to become more knowledgeable about the client's culture, values, or expressions. Studying current patterns or trends may be an imposed self-corrective movement.

Problem-solving provides a framework not only for self-managing professional investment, but also for examining the self-congruency of the client: what they attend to, the manner of attending, considering, adapting, and modifying levels of attentiveness in approaching challenge. What is the client expressing about values and cultural beliefs that are important in examining change? The problem-solving activity within the counseling session (without regard to the therapeutic models used for intervention) allows the clinician the opportunity to collect data, which provides information and insight into the client's social cognitive and environmental setting—the client-in-community context. From entry into the problem-solving dialogue through brainstorming culminating with reality-testing, the clinician is able to identify environmental, cultural, and behavioral values. You will be able to observe the range in personal investment that clients exhibit as they address personal challenges. Ethically, you want to help and cause no harm.

When working under supervision, make yourself accountable so you can maximize your skills. With your supervisor, develop questions and benchmark indicators of success. Your supervisor should be someone you trust who is skilled and invested in your professional development. It is always a good idea to allow yourself as many different types of supervising experiences as are possible and available to you.

Reflection

Is it possible to create a supervisor–supervisee relationship at any point with my practice?

You want to create learning experiences for yourself at any point in time. Your professional goal should include being a lifelong learner.

Ethics

Invest in understanding your professional role, taking into account what it involves and include specific ethics regulation updates to your discipline. Shared below are common ethical tenets we all have and use when working with the clinical problem-solving CMA. As you introduce the LIBRE Model problem-solving, share these principles with the client. They include:

- Respect—all persons involved in problem-solving are held in respect. Recognizing that this activity is open-ended vulnerability. It is important that the client feels comfortable to explore any/all social cognitive thoughts and behaviors.
- The clinician's responsibility is to manage the client's commitment to the problem-solving and the products of the problem-solving experience. There must be a mutual relationship that values the individual that neither demeans nor embarrasses anyone involved. Cultural perspectives must be identified and respected to promote the welfare of the client and the integrity of the provider.
- Client Safety—client safety is critical; the client should never feel harassed or uncomfortable with personal problem-solving exploration. If at any time the client does express discomfort, the service provider should stop to re-establish agreed upon parameters. Boundaries must be maintained. The client must feel safe when working with the clinician.

  Be aware of physical distance; monitor and maintain a comfortable distance between your client and yourself. An agitated client will not be comfortable in exploring change. Allow the client the time and space to regain a sense of control and safety, or ask (as would be appropriate, with care not to offend) if the client needs to take a break. Acknowledge and embrace client diversity; this information is important to establish safety.
- Safe environment—Session location is important: problem-solving case management sessions should occur in a relaxed setting. Ask clients whether they feel safe before beginning the problem-solving exchange. The service provider should deliberately monitor the safe environment as defined by the client. A comfortable setting will facilitate problem-solving. Without regard to service settings, whether an office, school, or

community setting, make sure the location provides a calming location in which to work.

- Confidentiality—The client must have the confidence in the processing exchange. One of the most important principles of the service provider-client relationship is confidentiality that allows the client to process difficult feelings without losing face and without fear of others knowing what has been shared.

  The service provider must champion confidentiality as much as possible in accordance with site and discipline requirements. This level of confidentiality can be accomplished in part by explaining what confidentiality is and how it will be maintained. One possible overt expression may include shredding processing notes taken during the session to assure the client that nothing will be shared outside the session. There is, however, one consistent breach in confidentiality that should always occur. This is in relation to client safety. As an example, physical abuse or other violations of law must be reported.

  Openness—The client should have the freedom to speak within a problem-solving environment. As the service provider identifies opportunity, the client is taught or reinforced through practice how to self-regulate. Problem-solving is designed to be instructional with the anticipation that the client will begin to independently solve problems and process challenges as a result.

  Independence—The client is encouraged to self-regulate. The clinician strives to help the client achieve independent function by teaching and providing feedback as the client learns how to apply acquired skills in daily life.

Reflection

Why is it necessary to address ethics prior to problem-solving?

Problem-solving is designed to slow down the thinking process to allow for uncensored considerations. Without the ethics to address boundaries, the client may not feel comfortable.

Boundaries in Working with a Client

Boundaries are safeguards, and for the more novice clinician, boundaries are training wheels to keep you from falling down or, in counseling, placing you at risk of either a legal or ethical claim. Boundaries protect you, the client, and the professional relationship. Begin by exploring your preferred boundaries. Think first about yourself and when you feel safe. Do you like to sit close to the person you speak with, or do you like distance to be maintained?

Do you like people to speak with you using a quiet voice? Are you challenged when approached by someone who is agitated? Are you OK when people yell or use a loud voice as they speak to you? Your awareness of personal boundaries will assist you as you prepare for your client.

You will likely notice that your interpersonal preferences carry over as you begin working with a client, so be aware of yourself. While you may initially want to match the client's engagement style to establish rapport, make sure that you are aware of your purposeful matching the client's engagement. Within the context of counseling, formal boundaries are critical. Use physical space between you and your client to concretely illustrate the boundaries and to assist you both with the mental and psychological space that compliments the working relationship. Meanwhile you will be monitoring these professional boundaries at all times.

Remember you are not visiting with a friend; you are providing an opportunity for skill development. For instance, the mirroring technique (matching tone and pace of speech of the client) may be helpful in establishing rapport and in tracking client comfort. The additional value is that your client will likely relax. Returning to the lifeguard analogy, a lifeguard will minimize close contact when attempting to save someone in distress to ensure that the drowning person will not jeopardize his life. He may wait until the individual is no longer fighting to come close or instead offer a life preserver or hook to pull the individual to safety.

Reflection

When it comes to ethics, what self-talk should I be mindful of?

Remember that ethics are intended to protect you and your client. Make sure never to extend beyond your defined boundary as a service provider. Your self-talk may include safety topics: Am I keeping my client safe; Am I keeping myself safe? Have I clearly explained the boundaries? Do my clients understand what will be reported and what will be maintained in confidence?

Client Safety and When to Report

There are several absolutes as a service provider. Safety is paramount. Causing no harm is an ethical principle that must always be upheld. It is of critical importance to know and understand when to report. These decisions are usually directly in line with suspected harm to self or others. Make sure that you identify your site mission, service role, legal and ethical requirements, and boundaries before seeing your first client.

In summary, the first preparatory investment involves you: your professional development plan, engagement style, and identity development. Care for others begins with self-care. Develop an intentional professional identity development plan that is specific with measurable goals that you and your supervisor (if applicable) can monitor.

Reflection

As I prepare for my client, what are my takeaway components to prepare myself?

Be mindful; know your ethical principles as components of your PDP. Be accountable; work under supervision or self-examination to achieve your goals. Be genuine with yourself and be open to feedback. See yourself as a lifelong learner.

You have been assigned your client. Do your homework in preparing for your client. Learn as much as you can about the referral and background information prior to the first session. Develop a host of customized questions to begin collecting background information. Active listening and open-ended questions facilitate your establishment of rapport and data collection in connecting with your client.

Practice Client Exercise

You have walked into the office of your agency only to be greeted by someone in distress in tone and behavior exhibited. What would you want to consider prior to speaking with the individual? How will you approach this session? Your boss has informed you that you have twenty minutes to prepare yourself.

NOTES

1. American Counseling Association, "ACA Code of Ethics," 2014, http://www.counseling.org/resources/aca-code-of-ethics.pdf; American Psychological Association, "Ethical Principles of Psychologists and Code of Conduct," 2010, http://www.apa.org/ethics/cod/index.aspx; National Association of School Psychologists, *Principles for Professional Ethics* (Bethesda, Maryland: National Association of School Psychologists, 2010); National Association of Social Workers, "Code of Ethics," 2008, http://www.socialworkers.org/pubs/code/code.asp.
2. Albert Bandura, "Toward a Psychology of Human Agency," *Perspectives on Psychological Science* 1, no. 2 (2006): 164–180.
3. Norma S. Guerra, "Illustrations of Engagement Styles: Four Teacher Candidates," *Teacher Education and Practice* 22, no. 1 (2009): 95–117; Norma S. Guerra, "LIBRE Model: Engagement Styles in Counseling," *Journal of Employment Counseling* 44, (2007): 2–10.

4. Carrie Furrer and Ellen Skinner, "Sense of Relatedness as a Factor in Children's Academic Engagement and Performance," *Journal of Educational Psychology* 98, no. 1 (2003): 148–162.

5. Norma S. Guerra, "Illustrations of Engagement Styles," 95–117.

6. Norma S. Guerra, "Illustrations of Engagement Styles," 95–117.

7. Albert Bandura, "Social Cognitive Theory: An Agentic Perspective," *Annual Review of Psychology* 52 (2001): 1–26.

Chapter 4

Referral and Client Preparation

Each time you assume a service provider role, it is important to examine the larger system context.

Objective: To understand how the Case Management Approach supports the development of client sessions, service plan development and the organizing of the intervention.

This chapter examines the client as an individual-within-community,[1] as a social cognitive agent,[2] an active participant in life. We begin with a discussion of the Case Management Portfolio (CMP) as the case folder where the clinical problem-solving CMA session documentations are maintained. The preparatory steps to consider when receiving a referral and conducting the first counseling session are examined. We spend some time examining the CMA, which is the counseling structure. We examine the CMA counseling session as a shared social cognitive experience in which the client and clinician each have distinct roles. To illustrate, we revisit our text client and close with considerations in developing the case plan. We examine considerations in approaching background questions.

Let's begin with the repository for all client case information. The CMP is the master client-clinician organizing portfolio. The portfolio will be used to track your engagement style calibration in response to your client's needs. Within this folder, you will keep your LIBRE Model exchanges, CMA content session notes, clinical data, and session reflections. Building on the self-reflection discussed in chapter 3, you have been preparing yourself as the service provider. We are now ready to direct our attention to the client.

The CMA is a shared experience between you and your client in which you self-regulate and manage your preferred engagement as a clinician, separate yet in relation to your client's expressed engagement style. By acknowledging your personal engagement preference and holding this style as a constant or calibrated adjustment, you will be better able to see the distinctions between your clients in relation to you. I offer the following example to begin addressing the notion of calibration. Assume for a moment that you are at a park and want to ride on the adult-size seesaw (a device for leveraging weight from one person to another person). You must account for your weight in relation to the other person. If you are a small woman and want to lift a heavy male friend, you must first calculate weight to accomplish the task. You first consider your weight and then that of your friend. The distinction of weight will determine how to approach the task. The seesaw analogy is used here to represent the counseling exchange and your friend's weight represents the client's motivation (attentiveness/engagement) to change. You as the counselor must consider your weight as motivation (attentiveness/engagement) to have the client change. Depending on the client's placement on the seesaw (motivation), your approach will need to be adjusted.

The explanation for why it is important to calibrate your engagement prior to seeing your client is to facilitate communication. Your attention, motivation, engagement style and that of your client may not be the same. It is important to understand the client's motivated need to change. To better address this understanding, the client's motivated need to change must separate from our motivated need for him to change. I must not let my motivated need to change the client tilt the client's weight and motivation to change.

You may wonder why the extra step to self-monitor, given that you are a trained or in-training professional. Let's begin with the first example: you have completed a problem-solving LIBRE Model activity and have assessed yourself as an actual engaged clinician (this is demonstrated in your initial and sustained attentiveness to detail throughout the entire problem-solving activity). Because you are actual engaged, you are inclined to see all of your clients as actual engaged. You assume they must be actual engaged; thus, their motivation to seek counseling. This, however, may or may not be the case. Your acknowledged actual engaged orientation has increased your self-awareness. You model self-regulation for your client to introduce the concept to her. She will in turn demonstrate her engagement preference in the completion of the problem-solving experience. She is given the space to be a separate individual. Recognizing your own engagement and that of your client allows you to see her without imposing your engagement preference. Now you will be able to better assess her strengths and experiences along with gaps she presents through the completion of the problem-solving exchange.

Reflection

The CMA is a shared experience. Does this mean that my calibration is my monitoring of myself and that I will have to accommodate and monitor myself with each client?

Yes. You will need to calibrate for each client. This is absolutely correct. You will need to take time to prepare prior to seeing each client. Your engagement adjustment will be in response to the client need and thus be the result of your calibration.

Returning to the explanation for the inclusion of the clinician's engagement into the CMA, the self-identified engagement information will assist you with a more clear orientation in preparation for your counseling session. Identifying your engagement and your client's engagement separately will facilitate awareness about the subtle differences in attention and persistence between you and your client. This will assist you in viewing your client's context as expressed data. The more objective view of the attentiveness/engagement data will facilitate the development of the intervention. The self-check is a calibration to identify your engagement style as it occurs apart from that of your client's engagement style. This exercise is completed each time before you see your client.

The second CMA component is your client's LIBRE Model engagement (attentiveness) information. While we will discuss how to assess engagement styles in chapter 7, for now, it is important to conceptualize and understand that you will always be actively involved in analyzing the two engagement characteristics, yours and your client's, to keep an open prospective to the client's directional intervention: does the client want to complete no action toward change or does the client want to take action toward change.

Defining Services

Each time you assume a service provider's role, it is important to examine the larger system context. It is your responsibility to know the organization's system and its parameters. For instance, if I am working in a community agency, what type of client will I be working with? Will I be working with children, the elderly, or individuals with disabilities? What is my reporting chain of command? What detailed information should I include in my CMP? What do I report, when, to whom, and how? What type of records do I keep? Where are they kept? How is FERPA (The Family Educational Rights and Privacy Act) ensured? What provisions are made to ensure the safety of the client? If I am working in a school, it is important for me to understand how I report the information collected from students and to whom. You should know what is to be held in confidence and under what conditions confidence is not to be maintained.

Reflection

If I am working in private practice, where do I obtain the answers to these questions?

In private practice, determine the level of services beforehand and the conditions under which these services will be offered. Consult with external resources, other colleagues, and professional associations for direction and support.

The Referral

The referral usually includes your client's name, age, background, and any additional information collected along with the request for services (reason for seeking counseling). Your facility and referring agency goals, your role parameters, and the service guidelines provide you information that will be used to process the referral. The expectation is that you will work with that defined structure. An example may assist here. Within a school setting, it will be important to review parental permission prior to counseling a child or underage adolescent. School-based services may dictate times within the day that are appropriate to see the student. Academic records may be available upon request.

Once you have reviewed all available information, begin with a self-check (your self-regulated safety net): What is my engagement style preference today? While you will have a preferred engagement style, depending on what is occurring within you personally that style may vary. Thus, there is importance in my preparing and adapting (to calibrate) to my client's engagement. This adjustment will assist to establish rapport, to better understand her context and to establish a strong working relationship.

Case in point, I have determined that I am goal-focused; my client exhibits a venting engagement. She only wants to talk about the problem. Am I willing and able to make the engagement adjustment to attend to her venting without my session goal? I do this to better establish rapport and so that she will know that I am listening to her. I also recognize that if I remain with her in a venting engagement, we will not accomplish any work. I must decide at what point I plan to introduce my session work. What will this transition look like? I must ask myself: Do I have experience with the identified concern, chronological age, expressed culture, and reported cognitive function? What diversity issues or considerations does this client introduce? Is the engagement style linked to culture or personal experience? Remembering my goal, I want to provide the client a meaningful experience. To accomplish this task, I must be aware of the balance between my client's motivation in coming forward to receive services and my motivation in wanting to help this client. What possible client-clinician engagement combinations could occur? I must prepare myself accordingly.

Reflection

What could result from a mismatch in engagement styles?

Client frustration, angry or you may experience the same feelings of frustration.

Client Preparation

Setting up for your first session. Once you have identified your engagement style preference, there are three main first-session goals as you prepare for the client contact. You will want to analyze and develop your strategy beginning with these 3Cs, which include chronological age, culture, and cognition.

The first C is Chronological age, in which you make communication adjustments. If you are speaking with a child, adjust your language to be understood by the child. The same if you are speaking with an adolescent or older adult. One additional chronological age consideration would be to ask if the client (in combination with his age) has had experiences that are unique and that may impact his age developmental level. Thus you may ask the referring individual or self-referred individual, what type of experience considerations should I make in speaking with my client? For instance, speaking with a child whose parents are both attorneys will require a different preparation and approach as opposed to a child whose parents have had no formal education. Your presentation will be different given the distinct social cognitive experiences that each client has had.

The second C is Culture, which prepares you to see the client-in-community as a person with values, principles, and experiences—likely different from yours and thereby requiring you to adjust yourself to be open to a different life experience. Defined as client fit, this involves a social cultural match to meet and be present for your client. This activity may involve researching the client's background experiences within the client's community, as well as the client's experiences as defined by the community that is providing the referral. In some cases, you may be able to complete this prior to the first meeting; in other cases, it may not be possible. Further, there may be times when you are called to complete additional outside research to acquire cultural information. This investment will assist you in providing a more informed client communication.

For example, Sally is referred to you for services because she cries every time someone attempts to talk with her. After you complete your calibration, you may want to first explore her background culture and experiences. If you find that this is the first time Sally has had to interact within a culture and community unlike her primary cultural experience, this information becomes important to better understand why she cries when approached by people different from herself. You are setting a tone of respect without judgment. Thus, you come with a distinct approach. This was the reason you were invited to visit with Sally in the first place. The decision is your clinical judgment and it is made after having conducted some background research. You know that you are coming from a different cultural and background experience. This has nothing to do with your skills as a clinician. Your professional decision is to have someone from Sally's cultural community or family introduce you to her and explain why you are meeting.

The third C is Cognition, which prepares you to be a cognitive match for your client. This involves developing subject-content (for example, introducing the subject of a hobby) that is introduced as new thought or question and is followed through to process with the clients as far as they are willing to process. If possible, your goal is to confirm your client's cognitive approach. Returning to Sally, if the challenge is that Sally is adapting to this new community, you will want to introduce salient factors in line with her cognitive level. You may select to invite a family member, and together the three (you, Sally and the family member) talk about what will be involved in counseling. Together the three of you generate examples of when counseling might assist. We anticipate that Sally would feel relaxed and be able to enjoy this new experience.

Cognitively oriented considerations may include some of the following:

- Is this person receiving special services within or outside a school setting?
- How would the client likely define the school experience?
- Has this person ever been tested or received a psycho-educational diagnosis?
- Is this person under the care of a physician?
- Is this person taking medication that may be impacting cognitive judgment?

If the client is cognitively below average or has an intellectual disability, problem-solving is not appropriate. A low-cognitive-functioning client will become frustrated with the cognitive demand required to problem solve. Observationally, if you find your client repeating herself rather than generating any new thoughts, it would be best to move away from the problem-solving activity. There are developmental and legal guidelines that need to be maintained to protect the client. The normal range of cognitive function is one important requisite to using the LIBRE Model problem-solving activity.

Reflection

If the referral provides only basic information, then should I begin to develop 3C questions to engage the client?

Yes. It will be important to make sure to address chronological age, culture, and cognition. Confirm your 3C information with the client. Socratic questions will facilitate this endeavor.

1. Chronological age—how old is my client? What educational experience has she had? What social or other experiences might she have had that could have cognitively impacted her chronological age?
2. Culture—what is the ethnicity of the client? What is the race? What is the cultural community background? How does the client community celebrate or grieve? Does the background of the client match the community the client resides in, and how long has the client been in this community?
3. Cognition—The client must have normal cognitive function for this problem-solving approach to be useful. It will be important to seek information about the client's cognitive adaptability and experience. A low-cognitive-functioning individual will not benefit from the metacognitive intricacy involved in problem-solving.

The 3C context is combined with any social cognitive, goal orientation, ZPD information, and self-regulation evidence provided. You will want to begin developing a general picture of who your client is. You will want to explore prior experiences, identified challenges and how your client responded; this in anticipation of what will be introduced within the counseling session.

Reflection

Why is it not appropriate to use a problem-solving approach with a low-cognitive-functioning client?

Someone who is limited (or low) in cognitive function may find it difficult to brainstorm. The person may perseverate (repeat something again and again) and become frustrated.

With background homework and a referral strategy, you are ready to meet your client. You want your initial meeting to be engaging and approached with open-ended questions. Examples of these open-ended questions may include the following: What's your favorite movie or video game? Do you have a favorite color? What is the best day you have ever had? Use the 3C information provided within the referral to assist you in developing the questions.

First Client Session

As a general guide, identify community values and begin with concrete questions and activities. Use this information in developing your questions that will open the dialogue. Depending on the amount of information and time that you have been provided to prepare for the first meeting, you will want to pace the session accordingly. If you are able to acquire a sufficient amount of information prior to meeting your client, you may still need to collect or confirm information. This may involve inserting closed-ended questions into your conversation.

First establish rapport and then casually place a closed-ended question with the intention of moving back to open-ended questions. Examples of client closed-ended questions may include the following: How old are you? Are you in school? Have you ever skipped a grade or failed a grade? The danger of offering too many closed-ended questions is that your session will begin to sound more like an interrogation. You want your client to feel comfortable. You are introducing yourself as someone who is available to assist in processing challenges and who is skilled and trustworthy. Thus, each session should begin with your defined role and service parameters with defined limitations.

Reflection

Under what circumstance is problem-solving best used?

Problem-solving works best with short-term services and/or with high-crisis motivated clients who are within a normal range of cognitive capacity.

Administer the problem-solving activity. In clinical problem-solving, a workable level of distress can heighten motivation. Often it is that feeling of being stuck that is the impetus for change. Problem-solving works for the individual-in-need. The urgency of need to meet an immediate resolution to a confounding challenge introduces the opportunity to self-reflect and to reach a resolution. Problem-solving is not new. As early as King Solomon's problem-solving exchange with the two prostitutes, we see the importance of introducing a fresh approach to a tormenting problem. In this case, Solomon addresses the need without moving the focus to himself. Let's examine the story as it begins with the challenge presented to King Solomon.

Listen for the clients' worldview and concern: This woman and I live in the same house, and I had a baby while she was there with me. The third day after my child was born, this woman also had a baby. We were alone; there was no one in the house but the two of us. During the night this woman's son died because she laid on him. So she got up in the middle of the night and took my son from my side while I, your servant, was asleep. She put him by her breast and put her dead son by my breast. The next morning, I got up to nurse my son—and he was dead! But when I looked at him closely in the morning light, I saw that it wasn't the son I had borne. The other woman said, No! The living one is my son; the dead one is yours.

Identify the Problem: Who is the Mother of the Living Baby?

> *Brainstorm:* The king said, This one says, My son is alive and your son is dead, while that one says, No! Your son is dead and mine is alive.
>
> Then the king said, Bring me a sword. So they brought a sword for the king.
>
> He then gave an order: Cut the living child in two and give half to one and half to the other.
>
> *Reality-test:* The woman whose son was alive was filled with compassion for her son and said to the king, Please, my lord, give her the living baby! Don't kill him!
>
> But the other said, neither I nor you shall have him. Cut him in two!
>
> *Encourage:* Then the king gave his ruling: Give the living baby to the first woman. Do not kill him; she is his mother.[3]

Data analysis and case plan generation. We pause here to summarize and analyze the exchange before continuing. The problem-solving approach sets the stage for a client's self-reflection, which includes social skills, knowledge, culture, and other parallel experiences.[4] Brainstorming introduces creative thought. Possible solutions to the identified problem will include social, cultural, cognitive, and emotional aspects. The client is providing possible and impossible, probable and improbable thoughts. There is natural client presentation introduced within this story. The client is providing you a range of divergent possibilities in resolving this challenge even before any reality-testing is undertaken. There is a simplistic elegance to problem-solving as the metacognitive facets of attention, self-reflection, and goal orientation.[5] The problem-solving process is a personalized and self-regulated investment to change in which individuals' frame their customized plan.[6] If the problem would not have been resolved and further counseling services needed, this would have been the point when the data would have been analyzed and the case plan with next steps developed.

Review of collected problem–solving units of information. In counseling, problem-solving allows the clinician to collect data and monitor client engagement, assist with the cognitive and cultural processing and monitor new adaptive client change. You will be able to assess and assist by first matching with the client's engagement and then, with rapport and defined parameters, you are able to introduce new modes, information or intervention models for adaptability and change.

With the problem-solving foundation, we move to the next step in preparing the case conceptualization. This involves the development of the case plan to set the direction, develop services, intervention and monitor progress (evaluation or feedback plan).

Intervention

The data collected from this initial exchange is invaluable, and it provides key information that can then be used to set up the initial case plan. Let's begin by defining need. From this, we can better understand what the case plan will provide and what we want to achieve in creating a client-centered services.

The case plan much like a hypothesis operates as a proposition or set of propositions that can be used to explain and frame direction.[7] In a clinical setting, the case plan need and direction generally come from the referral. The clinical problem-solving activity with the client facilitates identifying the challenge(s) and necessary support for the individual from the perspective of the client. This additional perspective assists with the development of decision making (goals) and the plans that would allow him to go forward to achieve positive gains. For us as service providers, the case plan is the rudder that sets the direction and becomes the case management goal from which we measure client gains and successes. As a clinician, it is important to work with the client in developing the plan. Inform the referring agency (as appropriate) to the developing case plan to make sure the identified interventions will be within the identified area of need. Counseling intervention services are developed from and for the established goal, either in response to the referral or in collaboration with those involved with the referral.

In the text case, the school referral was focused on grades, attendance, and Leah's graduation plan. Leah wants to live with her boyfriend and is concerned about her housing needs and her unborn baby. To meet both goals, your carefully crafted plan will address both concerns. Begin with one specific plan and if additional adjustments are warranted, make those changes. For example, the clinical case plan addresses a lack of skill and/or need. The plan may likely state that Leah does not have the academic time management skills (referral) or the personal support (client identified need) to be successful. The problem-solving skills are an underlying need to make better decisions, which can be used to link the two needs (school and outside concerns). If Leah is provided the academic time management and support with the underlying problem-solving to manage the identified needs, there is an increased probability that she will make better choices.

Reflection

What is the purpose of the case plan?

The purpose of the case plan is to focus on the referral-identified need and the client's targeted need. The combined deficit or lack of skill will then orient the intervention plans that will be developed to assist with the client's healthy growth and development.

In outlining the intervention, focus on the goal(s) addressed by the case plan. For example, teaching and practicing problem-solving or decision-making skills become the goal. These skills are then introduced and supported to meet each client-identified goal, which supports the focus of the case plan. Identifying the intervention and evaluation are then used to monitor client change. Address your criteria in measurable or observable terms. Create goals that will assist the client in moving forward in a positive adaptive direction. Questions to ask yourself may include: What would be an observable behavior related to this skill? For now, let's stay with a decision-making activity. The intervention preparation may include a task analysis. For instance, the client will be able to perform specific problem-solving sub-set skills. How will I measure these skills? You decide to create sub-activities that address the smaller subset skills needed to accomplish the problem-solving task. To extend this example, let us assume that the client subset skill is brainstorming. To measure acquisition of this brainstorming sub-set skill, you spend time with your client time practicing how to brainstorm. You define and practice with your client who learns to generate realistic and unrealistic options to a number of topics. This brainstorming is the measured intervention. Once your client learns to brainstorm you move to the reality-testing subset skill. Developing your evaluation plan at the same time as the intervention plan will assist you in measuring gains even as intervention activities are planned.

Reflection

Do I focus on the client's identified need or the referring agent identified need?

Ideally you want to frame your case plan and service intervention to meet the needs of both the client and the referent.

Intervention Evaluation: Monitoring Change

Measuring or rating gains and losses is important and this data should be included as CMA components. Consider developing formative (short-term and incremental) evaluations and summative (long-term) evaluations. With a larger goal, formative evaluation will allow you to monitor smaller changes. For instance, Leah may have formative evaluation criteria addressing her willingness to use a calendar or diary to keep up with the many changes she is experiencing. This time-management intervention activity involves a diary to monitor her school and personal time on a daily basis (formative evaluation). A summative evaluation may include making good decisions on a weekly basis for example, turning in assignments and visiting with teachers or counselors when she experiences challenges outside her control. An additional summative evaluation may include talking with her boyfriend and developing a plan for how best to manage their living situation. The formative evaluation plan would address how she will manage each day. The content of the developing skill is up to the client; you want to focus on the learned skill and its implementation.

Reflection

Should I be developing formative evaluation plans for each session and summative plans for key end points?

Yes, absolutely. For example, if a client is learning how to develop a goal, the formative evaluation may include components that make-up a strong goal (specificity and within the person's control); a second formative evaluation could then test on these points. A summative evaluation plan may be for the client to independently develop a strong goal.

Resiliency Plan

You will want to continue to develop additional questions to better understand cultural values (e.g., why she believes that remaining with her parents is not an option), chronological age (levels of responsibility she has experienced that seem to define how she sees herself) and her cognitive capacity (see Table 4.1). Asking questions is a great way to acquire information, but it is not the only way. Talking with teachers, parents, or others may also provide information about the 3Cs, social cognitive, goal orientation, ZPD, and self-regulatory experiences. With adults or older adults, these supportive systems may include friends and associated organizations that are in place to support the individual. With this in mind, do not feel like you must ask all of the questions you generate. The questions become your background brainstorming should you at some point feel stuck with how to proceed with your client. From this information, you will begin to construct a resiliency plan with the detail that is meaningful to the client. The background questions help her to begin thinking about the myriad of *what if* situations she may encounter.

Table 4.1 Background Questions by Developmental Age

	Initial Attention			*Sustained Attention*		
Age Groups	*Person*	*Environment*	*Behavior*	*Goals*	*Goal Planning*	*History of Goal Completion*
Children to Pubescent	What is your favorite toy? What do you like to do for fun? What food do you like to eat? What food don't you like?	Do you go to school? Do you have a best friend? Who do you play with or spend time with when you are at home?	What do you do when you are angry? What do you do when you are sad? What do you do when happy?	What do you want to be when you grow up? What do you like to do?	Do you have a plan? What is your plan? Have you ever been able to do what you like to do?	What goals have you reached? Has there ever been a goal you were not able to meet? Do you usually finish what you start?
Adolescent	What type of music do you like to listen to? What is your favorite TV show? What extra-curricular activities do you enjoy? What do you and your friends do for fun?	What school activities do you attend? With whom do you spend your free time? Do you have a favorite subject? When you're at home, who do you spend time with?	What do you do when you feel upset? Do you get upset often? What do you do when you feel happy? How do you react when you feel sad?	What are you going to do after high school? Do you want to go to college? What would you like to study? What do you want for a career? What other goals do you have? Any goals before graduate high school?	Do you plan to go to college? Have you selected a college? What is your plan for getting into your first-choice university? How will you accomplish the goals you've set for yourself?	What is your biggest accomplish ment this school year? What is a goal that you have reached? What goal unrelated to school have you reached? What is a goal you were unable to meet? Do you usually finish what you start?
Young Adult	Do you have a hobby? What do you spend your weekends doing? What is your favorite book? What hobbies do you have? What do you do for fun?	What do you do for work? Are you in school? With whom do you live? With whom do you spend your free time? Are you in a relationship?	How do you react when you feel anxious? What do you do when you are happy? What actions do you take when you get angry? What do you do when you feel sad?	Do you attend a university or college? Do you want to attend college? In what career do you see yourself? What goals do you have for yourself? What are your plans for the future?	What is your plan for maintaining the GPA you desire? What are your plans for getting into the field you want? What goals do you have for yourself for the next year?	What would you say is your biggest accomplishment to date? What goals related to school have you achieved? What goals not related to school do you have? What goals were you unable to meet? How did you adapt to not meeting them?

(Continued)

Table 4.1 *(Continued)*

	Initial Attention			*Sustained Attention*		
Age Groups	*Person*	*Environment*	*Behavior*	*Goals*	*Goal Planning*	*History of Goal Completion*
Middle Adults	What hobbies do you have? What is your favorite TV show? What do you do in your free time?	What is your job title? Are you married or in a relationship? Do you have any children? Do your children live at home? Do you live near your family?	What do you do to de-stress? How do you react when you feel angry? What do you do when you are sad?	What goals do you have for your career? What goals do you have for the next five years?	Do you have a plan for accomplish-ing your career goals? What is your plan for your five-year goals?	What goals have you already accomplished in your professional life? What goals have you reached in your personal life? What goals were you unable to reach?
Late Adults	What is your favorite daily activity? Do you have a hobby? What TV shows do you enjoy watching?	Are you married? Do you have children? Whom do you spend time with at home?	What do you do when you feel happy? How do you behave when you are sad? What do you do when lonely?	What goals do you have for the next few months? Any long-term goals?	Do you have a plan for reaching those goals? What actions are you taking to reach them?	What is your greatest professional accomplishment? What is your greatest accomplishment in your personal life?

Practice Client Exercise

Pi is a young person from another country who has been referred to you. Other than that this individual is old enough to provide consent, you have no additional information. How will you prepare to see this client? What will you do to assist this client? What is your plan for the first meeting? What would you intend to accomplish with this first session?

Calibrate your engagement and consider 3Cs context, social cognitive, goal orientation, ZPD, and self-regulation. How will you address each?

NOTES

1. Urie Bronfenbrenner, "Reaction to Social Pressure from Adults Versus Peers among Soviet Day School and Boarding School Pupils in the Perspective of an American Sample," *Journal of Personality and Social Psychology* 15, no. 3 (1970): 179–189.
2. Albert Bandura, "Social Cognitive Theory: An Agentic Perspective," *Annual Review of Psychology* 52 (2001): 1–26.
3. 1 Kings 3: 16–28 (New International Version).
4. Richard E. Mayer and Merlin C. Wittrock, "Problem Solving," in *Handbook of Educational Psychology*, 2nd ed. (Mahwah, NJ: Erlbaum, 2006): 287–303.
5. Daric R. Desautel, "Becoming a Thinking Thinker: Metacognitive, Self-Reflection, and Classroom Practice," *Teachers College Record* 11, no. 8 (2009): 1197–2020.
6. Norma S. Guerra, "LIBRE Stick Figure Tool: A Graphic Organizer to Foster Self-Regulated Social Cognitive Problem Solving," *Intervention in School and Clinic* 44, no. 4 (2009): 229–233.
7. Dale H. Schunk, *Learning Theories: An Educational Perspective*, 5th ed. (Upper Saddle River, NJ: Pearson, 2008).

Chapter 5

The First Client Session

LIBRE Model

Problem-solving is exemplified within the counseling interaction, as the client remains congruent and authentic in order to explore challenges with the intention of finding a resolution.

Objective: To learn the administration detail of the Listen-Identify-Brainstorm-Reality-test-Encourage (LIBRE) problem-solving Model.

This chapter addresses the LIBRE Model problem-solving administration, which can be used as a brief therapeutic approach alone or in combination with other therapeutic interventions (see Table 5.1). We revisit the text client. Please note that we repeat the details of the referral and Leah's story to call your attention to the flow of the session and LIBRE Model administration without being drawn into the content.

Problem-solving is a multifaceted activity. It is a metacognitive (having conscious awareness of one's thinking) exchange, with built-in intervals designed to pause the thinking to encourage a divergent (creative) to a convergent (reality-based) processing of a problem with the intention of reaching a resolution that has not been able to be reached previously. Problem-solving is exemplified within the counseling interaction, as the client remains congruent and authentic in order to explore challenges with the intention of finding a resolution. The LIBRE Model is a problem-solving approach , which consists of:

L: Listen to the client's identified worldview and list current challenges
I: Identify a specific concern
B: Brainstorm realistic and unrealistic options to solve the problem
R: Reality-test all plausible options
E: Encourage, which involves two prompted cues (first, the invitation to develop an action plan and second, an opportunity to create a timeline for the accomplishments of the scripted plan)

Table 5.1 LIBRE Model Stick Figure Tool Prompts

LIBRE Steps	*What is Your Prompt with this Stage?*	*What Will Happen Within this Stage?*
Listen	Let's talk about what's going on with you. I will list/record everything you tell me. What concerns are you experiencing? What is going on (with you)?	Facilitator prompts the client with the question and then records the client's response. This information is written on the *hair* of the LIBRE Model Stick Figure Tool.
Identify	Of everything you have identified as concerns, which one would you like for us to explore during this time together? If you made that concern into a question, what would that question be?	Participant identifies one concern and develops a question. For example, *What can I do to handle my stress?* Facilitator records the question on the shoulders of the LMSFT.
Brainstorm	In response to the question you identified, list all possible solutions you can think of, making sure that you say everything you think of whether it's realistic or not.	Facilitator offers open-ended questions to encourage the participant's exploration of options for addressing the identified concern. This listing is scribed on the *left side of the body*.
Reality-test	Let's now eliminate all nonworking options by crossing them out. Of those remaining, if you did complete this action, what would it look like?	Facilitator works with the participant in exploring consequences (positive and negative) involved in pursuing each option. The responses to *what it would look like if the option were completed* are written on the *right side of the body*.
Encourage	There are three parts to this step: (1) list the steps to your best solution, (2) what is the timeline for each step, and (3) what word would you offer yourself as encouragement for the completion of this activity?	Facilitator affirms with restatements and summaries. Facilitator re-states the ground rules of a safe, respectful, and confidential opportunity to explore the self-identified problem or concern. Response to (1) is written on the *left foot*; (2) is written on the *right foot* and (3) is under the LMSFT.

The LIBRE Model exchange closes with a summary. The client is asked to think of a positive word or mantra that provides an affirmation. This personalized word or phrase is designed to encourage the client to sustain investment in the problem-solving plan that has been developed. This self-initiated statement provides one final supportive boost.

The LIBRE Model five-step prompts are open-ended to encourage client dialogue. The client is invited to offer thoughts, feelings, and associated expressions. The content of this dialogue is solely the responsibility of the client. The client is free to speak to any subject. This dialogue then becomes the foundation for the CMA counseling experience. The collected data comes from the client's words and expressions to set a framework for future exchanges. The client's words and detail in content presented are the data points that are analyzed to determine engagement styles. It is essential that only the client's words be recorded. Visualize this exchange as taking a picture of your client: where the client is in the moment (the surrounding environment), what is of importance to the client, and who is of importance to the client are all elements of your picture. You are taking a snapshot of the client-in-the-moment. In reflection ask, how useful would this snapshot be if I placed myself in front of the client? With your face in front of your client, whom would you see? Thus, there is importance of recording only the client's words.

To assist with recording of the problem-solving, the LIBRE Model Stick Figure Tool (LMSFT) was developed. This LMSFT is a graphic organizer and visual reference for the client. As the service provider and the client work in partnership, the clinician shares the prompts then records the client's responses on the stick figure. It was with this partnership in mind that the stick figure graphic was created. The underlying idea for the stick figure was to use a record format that looked familiar. Most cultures and children have experience with stick figure drawings. In terms of modeling, the client should be able to view the care that the clinician assumes in recording each response. This implied courtesy is intended to allow the client to relax so that she may feel comfortable to self-reflect and self-regulate attentiveness as she speaks to the challenges at-hand.

The following LIBRE Model exchange is restated to present the administration from beginning to close. The intention is to highlight the process without distracting with new client content.

Referral Information

Reason for Referral: Upon Leah reporting to her teachers that she is pregnant, she has been referred for services. The referral is to address the problem of absenteeism and her drop in her GPA from those absences.

Background Information: Leah is a sixteen-year-old first-generation Mexican-American girl. Neither of her parents went to school beyond sixth grade, so they were pleased that she decided to remain in school. She is now in high school with plans to graduate next year. She is bright and does well in school. Her family has no long-term goals for Leah and she does not have any for herself, so finishing high school is a great goal. In doing so, she will be the first in her family to graduate from high school. Her parents told her they love her; however, they will not allow her to live at home if she plans to keep seeing the father of her baby. They believe it is time for her to begin her new life for her boyfriend and baby. As a result, Leah has decided to move in with her boyfriend, who dropped out of school and is prepared to support her and their baby.

Clinician Referral Processing: As a trained or in-training clinician, you have prepared for this initial exchange. You have reviewed the 3Cs and developed additional questions to collect social cognitive data that will supplement the background information. This includes:

- Clinician Self-Assessment and Calibration: assessed engagement style (Calibration of engagement style to better assist client) is goal-focused, so you will monitor not rush the client.
- Referral—examined data provided.
- Client preparation: developed 3C questions—Chronological age: Leah is sixteen years old, and her parents did not achieve the academic experiences that she has achieved. Culture: Leah is Mexican-American and has lived in the United States most of her life. Cognition: Leah is reported to be of above average-to-average intelligence.
- First Client Session—LIBRE Model Activity—prepared with a copy of the LIBRE Model as your initial activity and data collection protocol.

Begin with an introduction, restating that you have a signed consent from her parents and that you are now invested in securing her assent (approval) before going forward with this meeting. She agrees to speak with you; the session begins. You talk briefly about school and other activities that she is involved in and outside of school. Leah is relaxed and says she is happy to be speaking with you because she has something on her mind and did not know where to go with her thoughts. You see this as the perfect opportunity to introduce the LIBRE Model, so you begin by explaining that you have a problem-solving activity if she wants to try using it.

She agrees. You begin by explaining the conditions of confidentiality that will be maintained and the instances when you will be required to report. She nods, so you confirm by asking her if she understands.

LIBRE Model ethical ground rules are presented as below:

1. Respect: maintain respect and trust as the client explores concerns
2. Safety and Safe Environment: afford the client a secure setting
3. Confidentiality: allow the client the freedom to process concerns without losing face
4. Openness and Independence: encourage a sense of openness to problem solve with the anticipation that the problem-solving may be completed independently in the future

LIBRE Model Problem-Solving Activity Begins

She listens to your presentation. You introduce the LMSFT and clarify that you will record all of her responses. You further explain that this will be her opportunity to define a problem-solving goal. She sees the graphic organizer and you begin to speak with the first prompt (informing her that you will be recording her responses on the head of the LMSFT):

L: Listen

Let's talk about what is going on (with you) right now. I will list everything you tell me. What concerns are you experiencing?

Leah shares that she and her boyfriend are going to have a baby; they are very excited. She wants to finish school but the biggest problem she has is her living conditions. Her boyfriend quit school so they could have their own place, but now her boyfriend's mother has moved into their apartment. Leah explains that she is OK with the mother moving in because she had promised to help with the rent; however, now the mother's boyfriend is living with them and it has been months and no one is helping her boyfriend with the rent. You record her challenges within the L section (hair) of the LMSFT.

I: Identify

Transitioning Directions: we now move to the identify section where the responses will be added to the LMSFT shoulders.

Begin the second prompt: Of everything you have identified as concerns, which one would you like for us to address during this time together? If you were to write the concern as a question, what would the question be?

Leah replies: What can I do to support my boyfriend?

B: Brainstorm

Transitioning Directions: we now move to brainstorming, which is recorded the left side of the LMSFT body.

In response to the question you identified, list all possible solutions you can think of, and let's make sure that you think of realistic and nonrealistic solutions. The reason behind encouraging the client to generate realistic and unrealistic options is to cultivate new and creative thought without regard to the commitment to act on any option generated.

Leah is motivated by the care you have exhibited, including writing down only her exact words, so she continues to dictate: I could tell the mother's boyfriend to leave. I could tell the mother to leave. She pauses. I could leave. I could do nothing. I could talk with my boyfriend about how we need to talk with his mother and her boyfriend.

Transitioning Directions: once the brainstorming has been completed, you will want to ask the client to eliminate any non-applicable options and those that may be good options but that are not of interest to the client. Have the client x out those options. Follow-up by asking the client to prioritize the remaining options.

Let's now eliminate all non-preferred options by crossing them out. Then, of the remaining, if you did complete an action, what would that action look like?

Leah smiles. That is easy. I know I can't tell the mother's boyfriend to leave, so that is not going to happen. I'm also not going to tell the mother to leave either. She continues, saying that she loves her boyfriend and he loves her, so she has no intention of leaving him. Leah smiles. I know that I am going to do something. That leaves me with my last solution. I am going to talk with my boyfriend. When asked to prioritize, she reiterated: (1) I am going to talk with my boyfriend.

Transitioning Directions: Now moving to the reality testing, you will ask the client to further develop the remaining brainstormed option. You will ask the client to explore any associated actions that may be required to go forward with the brainstormed option.

R: Reality-test

Let's now further examine the remaining options. If you were to go forward with the remaining option or options (as appropriate), what would that look like? You want the client to behaviorally step-through next steps.

Leah is quick to reply. If we sit down and decide what exactly needs to be said, then I can support him in how he needs to talk with his mother and her boyfriend.

Transitioning Directions: Take the time to summarize the client's thinking that has occurred up to this point. Restate the listening, identifying, brainstorming, and reality-testing roles and purposes. It is important for the client to see how this problem-solving process has intentionally slowed down the thinking to further develop the distinction between thinking and doing as two separate processes.

E: Encourage

List the steps to your best solution. Responses are recorded on the left foot of the LMSFT.

Leah begins: I need to ask my boyfriend to meet me at the grocery store so we can talk. Then we can decide what we are going to tell his mother and her boyfriend. We will need to decide what we are going to do if they don't pay anything; that way if we need to move we can begin planning what we need to do. We could look for another apartment and be ready to move in two months.

What is the timeline for each step? Responses are recorded on the right foot of the LMSFT.

Leah: Today, I am going to ask him to meet me at the grocery store. Today, we can practice what we are going to tell his mother. The apartment is under her name. By that time we will need to make new arrangements. Leah is referencing the time and plans they would have to make to move. If we need to move, then we can do it next month. If we follow our plan, we should be in our new apartment within two months.

Transitioning Directions: now that the problem-solving has been completed, it is important to see the process as a whole. Ask the client to self-reflect and to encourage self.

What word would you offer yourself as encouragement for the completion of this plan?

Leah: We can do this! We have options to move forward!

You close the session by asking her how she feels about what was discussed. She replies that she is excited about her plan. You give her a copy of the activity and set up a meeting for next week.

When you meet with her next week, include a revisit of this initial plan to determine if the plan was completed. Explore only as much as the client is open to sharing. In terms of counseling sequence, it is best to complete a mood check-in first (How are you doing? How are things going?). Once you determine that the client is comfortable and ready to work, review the last session's LIBRE Model plan. This exchange will provide a summary of your last visit and assist with the introduction to your newly planned activity. It is at this point that additional counseling techniques may be integrated into the CMA. For example, if time management is identified as an intervention need. You are now ready to introduce a new skill or reinforcing exercise to practice the identified developing skill. Monitor the client's skill development and look for opportunities to reintroduce these skills as you continue the exchange. The session will pass quickly. Pace the interaction and dialogue to the client's preference and allow time to restate gains so that the client is able to see you modeling self-reflection and self-regulation.

Observe your client's engagement. As the working relationship develops, you may find that you want to introduce engagement into your counseling session communication. I would recommend that you wait until you have had your client complete several LM SFTs. These worksheets assist with the details of the content discussed and the engagement style (identified attentiveness while problem-solving). You will want to confirm your observations by asking your client for feedback. At this point, present copies of all of the completed LMSF worksheets so that she is able to see her different response patterns. Your presentation may include an overview of the four engagements and a discussion of how and when each is an efficient engagement style.

Always have an agenda with each meeting. Focus your intervention and offer an activity with time to reflect, learn, and for practice. Leave time for closing (leaving your client with a positive word of encouragement). Build your client's self-efficacy, allowing her to see her learned problem management skill.

Thus, Leah is an example of what an actual engagement dialogue looks like; now, let's examine the remaining three engagement styles. While the LIBRE Model prompts and transitional directions remain the same, the client responses will vary as note with the following three remaining engagement style examples.

Potential Engagement

A potential engagement session may include a referral. For example, Sandra is nineteen years old and lives with her mother and father. She is now in college and has been experiencing a large number of challenges. Her friends suggest she come to the counseling center. You have been assigned this case. No other information has been provided. You have calibrated your engagement style and are ready to receive your client.

You invite her into the initial session. After attempting to secure additional information with limited success, you decide to ask Sandra if she would be interested in a problem-solving activity. She nods her head; you introduce the LIBRE Model after explaining the ethics of what to report and ground rules involved with the activity.

LIBRE Model Problem-Solving Activity Begins

You open the dialogue with the L: Listen prompt.

Let's talk about what is going on right now. I will list everything you tell me. What concerns are you experiencing?

Sandra shrugs her shoulders, not much.

After prompting her for additional information, you move to the next prompt, I: Identify.

Is there a specific concern that you would like to address?

Sandra shrugs her shoulders again but, this time she says, I don't really have any specific problem and when I do, I always talk with my mother and she tells me what to do.

You make an effort to engage Sandra in any dialogue about school, friends, or home. Each time, Sandra indicates that all is going well. Finally after stepping through each of the remaining prompts, you close the activity. You ask her again about her visit to the counseling center. She says, there is a lot going on but she really can't talk about it right now. You immediately move to ask her to offer herself a positive word or words for having come to visit and talk with you today. She pauses and says *I can do this*! You thank her as you repeat her positive words back to her – you can do this! And let her know that you are there should she decide to talk about her specific challenges.

She says, thank you and leaves.

The potential engagement, from the beginning to close, is observable as a filtered communication. Sandra was careful not to share any information. Thus in terms of data collected, you are able to report the visit, the filtered communication, flat affect, and in terms of microsystems, Sandra is very closely tied to her family and that family system. You have the initial information indicating that Sandra is experiencing a number of challenges and should she decide to return for counseling, you may want to explore the family system. She may not be able to speak with you because she has not been able to ask her mother for permission. You generate a series of questions, should she return before closing the case.

Venting Engagement

The venting engagement style presents as a variation of the actual and potential engagements. This individual enters the session very engaged, however, the attentiveness is not sustained. This was the case of Maria, a fifty year-old woman who had been married for 30 years and until recently has been living in Mexico. Her husband who was a U.S. citizen had been living in the United States where he has lived and worked to provide for his family. He has always been faithful to go to Mexico to be with his family on the weekends and holidays. Together they have two children. Now that the children are grown and have married, Maria decided to come to live with her husband in the United States. However, when she arrived, she found that he had another family. You received this case because you speak both English and Spanish. You have calibrated your engagement style and are ready to receive your client. After the appropriate salutations and counseling protocol, you decided to offer Maria the LIBRE Model. She agrees; the reporting ethics and ground rules are shared.

LIBRE Model Problem-Solving Activity Begins

L: Listen

Let's talk about what is going on right now. I will list everything you tell me. What concerns are you experiencing?

Maria is quick to explain her visit as she begins to cry, I love my husband, and we have been married for 30 years. I thought once the children were grown and married that it would be OK for me to come and live with my husband but when I arrived, I found that he has a seventeen-year-old daughter. The mother of the girl is gone but that girl . . . she calls my husband "Daddy." She is a mean girl too. She makes a big mess with the expectation that I pick everything up after her. She treats me like her maid and my husband . . . all he does is say, I'm sorry. Then he goes on to say, she is his daughter and she has no one else but him. Maria pulls out a tissue to wipe her tears as she softly cries.

You ask if there is anything else she would like you to record. When she nods her head and says, no; you continue with the second prompt.

I: Identify

Of everything you have identified as concerns, which one would you like for us to explore during this time together?

I want to talk about whether I should stay with my husband.

You explain that for the purposes of this exercise, you will want to create a question. She nods and together you restate her concern as a question: Should I stay with my husband?

You explain that you will now only focus on this question and to do so will need to brainstorm all possible and impossible options so that she does not limit her thinking. She nods her head in agreement.

B: Brainstorm

In response to the question you identified, list all possible solutions you can think of, and let's make sure that you think of realistic and nonrealistic solutions.

I love my husband but I could divorce him.

I could stay and make him tell the girl to leave.

I could do nothing.

I could go back to Mexico and talk with my children.

I could go talk with my Priest.

She begins to cry again and then tells you that she cannot think of anything else. You ask her to eliminate those options she knows she will not follow-up. She only eliminates—doing nothing.

R: Reality-test

You notice a change in how she addresses this cue. She has stopped crying. She explains in detail what her actions would be if she acts on each. She begins with divorcing him to making him tell the girl to leave. The girl really does not have anyone but my husband and she is still a child. She is angry and feels betrayed like me. I think I need some time and space. Maybe going back to Mexico is the best I can do. At least then, I can go and sit and talk with my children and explain the entire situation to them. I guess they may have some ideas too. My Priest is always there for me. I think I need to go to church and spend time praying about this too.

You explain that the next step involves developing an action plan. Up to this point, we have only been processing options. You tell her that the purpose of the exercise is to slow things down so that the necessary time to process is made available.

She smiles and says, I think I would like to stop here. I am not prepared to make any decisions. I need more time to think. Thank you.

You give her a copy of her LMSF worksheet and explain how she can fill in the remaining sections when she is ready. You immediately move to summarize her work and ask her to provide a word or statement of encouragement.

She smiles and says, God will help me with this! I do love my husband!

You thank her for coming in and let her know that you are there when she is ready to visit again.

While the session ended, you have been able to collect a great amount of information about her social cognitive thoughts, microsystem and ecosystem. You were not surprised when five months later she came to visit again. This second visit was as an actual engagement as she explained that she was going to stay with her husband and work with him to raise the girl. There are many variations to the venting engagement style but the consistent elements are the great detail with the Listen, Brainstorm and Reality-testing in combination with no resolution plan.

Goal-Focused Engagement

There is one final LIBRE Model report engagement style and that is the goal-focused responder. This person begins the activity much like the potential engaged person; however, once a topic of specific concern is identified, the individual becomes quite animated. Such was the example with Matthew. He had decided to change careers and had gone to the counseling center because he was feeling overwhelmed with all of the changes. You are assigned this client who also has come as a self-referral. You are taking him as a walk-in so you have had minimal time to do any background research. You have calibrated your engagement style and are ready to receive your client.

LIBRE Model Problem-Solving Activity Begins

L: Listen

Let's talk about what is going on right now. I will list everything you tell me. What concerns are you experiencing?

Not much, I am just feeling overwhelmed. I have not been to a doctor in over 20 years and I am beginning to think that may I need to.

You ask him if there is anything else that is going on and he says, no. You explain the next step is to identify a specific concern.

I: Identify

Of everything you have identified as concerns, which one would you like for us to explore during this time together?

His reply is immediate, I really only have one concern and that is that I need to see a doctor but I don't know how to identify a good doctor. You ask him to create a question so that the remainder of their time can be focused on that question. Matthew says how do I identify a good doctor?

B: Brainstorm

In response to the question you identified, list all possible solutions you can think of, and let's make sure that you think of realistic and nonrealistic solutions.

I could just pick a doctor from the telephone book.

I could talk with friends and ask who they see.

I could go online and look up doctors within the area.

I might even just ask my neighbor.

I might just forget about it.

I might set-up criteria and then interview several doctors.

R: Reality-test

Let's now eliminate all nonworking options by crossing them out.

I'm not going to pick a doctor from the telephone book. (X)

I guess I could talk with friends and ask who they see.

I also see myself going online and looking up doctors within the area.

I am not going to ask my neighbor. (X)

And I am not going to just forget about it. (X)

I definitely will begin setting-up criteria and then interview several doctors.

You explain that the next step involves prioritizing the remaining items. Matthew indicates and lists his priorities. Then, of the remaining, if you did complete an action, what would that action look like?

1. I definitely will begin setting-up criteria and then interview several doctors. As a matter of fact, I am going to look up online possible criteria for selecting a good doctor and create my own checklist.
2. I also see myself going online and looking up doctors within the area. I might also look at doctors near my work so that if I ever need to leave work because I am not feeling well, I can quickly arrive.
3. Once I have my questions, I am going to ask my friends whom they see and ask them why they like their doctors and ask for additional interview questions.

Once he is finished reality testing, you ask him if he would like to develop an action plan. Up to this point, we have only been processing options. You tell him that the purpose of the exercise is to slow things down so that the necessary time to process is made available. He is very excited to go forward and nods, yes let's draft a plan.

E: Encourage

List the steps to your best solution.

1. I need to set-up some time to go online and do some research.
2. Then I will write out my interview questions
3. Ask my friends about their doctors
4. Go online and identify doctors in my area and close to work
5. Then begin setting up interviews with those that meet the close to work and area criteria and make sure to include any that my friends might recommend.

What is the timeline for each step?

I will take care of (1) and (2) tonight after work. Tomorrow, I will take care of (3) and (4). I will then be ready to begin setting-up appointments and interviews next week until I find the perfect doctor.

You now ask Matthew, What word would you offer yourself as encouragement for the completion of this plan?

His reply, I am ready!

You close the session by asking him how he feels about what was discussed. He says that he is very excited and feels great. He also explains how helpful this has been and asks if he may come again because he has other things that he would like to talk about too.

You say of course and set-up a time for next week.

Practice Client Exercise

You prepared your background questions from the limited information provided. You decided to use the LIBRE Model to collect additional information. Use the LMSF worksheet to conduct your first session problem-solving activity.

Chapter 6

Data Analysis and Case Plan Generation

Clinical Problem-Solving

Facing problems facilitates a personal balance; there is a confidence and emotional release when the person addresses what was once too challenging.

Objective: To investigate how to use clients' problem-solving information in developing the intervention treatment plans.

While much has been written about problem-solving,[1] this chapter presents problem-solving as it contributes to the CMA. The client's data is used to identify and analyze a need. The LIBRE Model client responses structure the contextualized and targeted interventions. The case plan is revisited regularly and refined as needed to meet identified or changing client needs. Beyond the initial referral, interventions are developed to include social cognitive learning opportunities with behavioral outcome measures to benchmark gains. Anticipated challenges and identified strengths round out the client's portfolio to provide an ongoing record of each client session. Client progress is documented, and self-regulated resilience plans are developed as a closing component prior to the client termination of services.

To review, we always begin with researched background information, 3C responses, and data collected about the client's social cognitive experience, goal orientation, and willingness to develop resolution plans. The client's words are the data used to provide insight and information. As clinicians, we will attend to client consistency as a measure of congruency and commitment to change.

Problem-solving literature provides a basis for this clinical examination. Skilled problem-solving involves the internal construction of knowledge such that the solver is able to organize the quality, specificity, and coherence of what is known to resolve unfamiliarity associated with an identified challenge (see Figure 6.1). The proficient problem solver exhibits increased on-task goal-setting behavior and task persistence.[2] Unskilled problem-solving is difficult, requiring large amounts of time and effort and it may not produce the desired result. Unskilled problem solvers are likely to give up, using statements that suggest the unavailability of options toward resolution or change. Unskilled problem solvers will likely revert to prior social cognitive management of conflict. These distinct data patterns have been found in expert-novice problem solver studies.[3] As clinicians we can use problem-solving skills as an ideal entry into the counseling exchange. The client's need is a significant consideration because what is identified within the referral may not be the client's need.

By assuming this CMA, we are able to assess the client's social cognitive and goal-oriented worldviews. This information is then condensed into trajectories from which a working plan is designed. For example, if we address the problem-solving activity with the goal of better understanding the client's worldviews and find that he does not respond, we may then want to explore further through observation (outside the problem-solving activity) to identify relevant social cognitive skills and experiences. Thus, the CMA helps to identify the client's self-managed experience and attentiveness through the observed problem-solving experience to begin the intervention. It is the client who defines the challenge and the client who defines the level of self-management toward change. The client content is expressed in response to the problem-solving prompts. The strength-based problem-solving activity LIBRE Model has the goal of identifying challenges and resolutions.[4] This process-product approach assists in the structuring of challenging experiences that determine additional instructional or intervention support.

To illustrate how the LMSFT is used as a graphic organizer with five prompts—Listen, Identify, Brainstorm, Reality-test and Encourage—and as the protocol for data collection, we revisit our text client, Leah, and walk through the processing steps.

Data Analysis

The LIBRE Model works best with individuals who have probable self-awareness and are experiencing a challenge. In Leah's case as a high school student, she has experienced academic success and has been productive in class. These academic successes should be noted as strengths. Further, it was the change that occurred in her academic behavior and performance that operated as the impetus for referral. The information on which we focus assists with the development of the treatment plan and intervention.

The service provider asked how best to assist her without highlighting her stark behavioral changes. Leah was given the opportunity to identify her concerns within her own personalized worldview. Goal setting and planning facilitate action,[5] components found within the LIBRE Model dialogue that help her sustain interest in developing a resolution. Process approaches such as the LIBRE Model provide for cognitive consistency or cognitive consonance as described by Festinger.[6] Leah was able to speak to her concerns without interruption and to examine her values and behavior as they are challenging her at the moment. For her to be cognitively consistent, she had to either change her values about school success or the living arrangement challenge. Facing problems facilitates a personal balance; there is a confidence and emotional release when the person addresses what was once too challenging.[7] The design of the LIBRE Model activity encourages active participation, and client-centered dialogue assists with the establishment of rapport and provides an outlet for addressing potentially overwhelming challenge. By having the service provider record the responses, Leah was able to see the challenge she was experiencing in her current state of imbalance.

LIBRE Model Data Elements

Listen Cue

The Listen prompt provides the client opportunity to address personal values and priorities. Deci, Vallerand, Pelletier, and Ryan[8] assert that there is more investment with control distinctions in self-determination of options. In the case of the LIBRE Model, this prompt encourages the individual to express any and all worldview concerns using her own language and expression. In analyzing the information provided, detail is the focal point of analysis. An attentive person will offer a larger number of different concerns with greater detail as compared to the student who is not self-aware or who is less attentive. Thus, the two key elements are (1) number of distinct items identified, and (2) level of specificity. Leah's theme was linked to her support for her boyfriend. She identified eight items in response to the Listen cue; however, the concerns addressed her current living situation. The specificity of distinct items (expressed across the eight data points) suggests self-awareness. Six of the items addressed distinct areas of concern with the remaining two supporting the identified six concerns.

Here is our data in response to the Listen cue:

1. Home environment: her living condition is her largest concern (she no longer lives at home with her family of origin). She is living with her boyfriend, his mother and her boyfriend.
2. Personal value: Leah remains committed to finishing school.

3. Personal commitment: she is going to have a baby.
4. Social Imbalance as justice/injustice: her boyfriend quit school; his mother and her boyfriend moved in, and only Leah's boyfriend is paying rent.

Identify a Concern

A personal goal is identified with this prompt. The self-managing individual who is motivated will likely offer specificity in the concern. The requested question will be detailed and within the individual's control. The individual who is not attentive to self (or does not self-manage) will find it difficult to move forward with a specific question. Generating a specific question may appear to be an impossible task. This client will want to be told what to do rather than to create an individual goal. With the case of Leah, her question is clear and definitive: What can I do to support my boyfriend? She appears to be cognitively balancing her values with her goal. This information provides a direction for both the service provider and Leah. Their focus is now the direction that will be assumed as they prepare to go forward with the intervention. Because the service provider is not offering any direction, there is intentional open-ended language to allow Leah time to think and consider possible strategies. Only after the LIBRE Model activity has been completed would the clinician's input be provided. This input would generally include an affirmation for the initiative to problem solve and if the generated resolution plan was flawed or held potential harm to self or other, then additional reality-testing or role play would be introduced.

An analysis of this Identify a concern response suggests that Leah is willing to continue. There is implied commitment and investment in resolving this identified challenge. She created a discrete goal with a question that has the potential of producing a particular solution. The goal she identified is within her control. This is suggestive of someone who is motivated and likely to persist.

Brainstorm

In analyzing brainstormed information, the clinician is looking for client investment and creativity in divergent and convergent options to resolve the identified question. If only realistic options are provided, then only limited exploration has been provided. This occurrence is found when the individual does not know how to brainstorm or feels uncomfortable brainstorming. In Leah's case, she provided five brainstormed options; four were unrealistic and one was realistic. All items were examined; four were eliminated. The remaining option was the only prioritized option, so that was then the thread of investment carried through to reality-testing. This profile suggests investment and willingness to explore change in behavior to resolve an identified concern. Her language appears to reflect thoughtfulness and focus. She seems to reflect her values and beliefs about what is possible and impossible. She eliminates the impossible options for her. For example, telling her boyfriend's mother to leave. This response offers information that reflects Leah's cultural and other social cognitive values, which the clinician notes and will discuss at a later time.

Reality-Test

Data provided by this component addresses the continuity of investment in the priority as determined by the client. How willing was she to follow through with solutions generated? Did she offer detail about her solution? In analyzing this information, new information is also important. If the individual begins to repeat a response, this is suggestive of someone who is no longer interested or like not to pursue change. The repetition is suggestive of a lack of motivational focus, investment or lack of skill. The clinician is attentive to the language used by the client and levels of personal responsibility suggested. Does the reality-testing introduce potential harm to self or others? Are the steps logical? Is new information included? Are there cues that suggest the client is struggling with what might be involved behaviorally? In Leah's case, her remaining step offered additional detail in when and where she will find time to meet and talk with her boyfriend. There is some generality to her response that suggests she is still processing what that would look like. There is a transitioning point of the LIBRE Model activity as the person moves from the reality-testing to the encourage step.

Clients are asked to ponder options up to this point in the process (no actions are requested). The encourage step invites the client to move from thinking about action into developing an action plan. Here the client may select to incorporate any of the thoughts developed into an action plan or decide to take a different direction (using none of the resolution thoughts developed thus far). Some clients may ask you to repeat the explanation of process and others may ask you to define reality-testing. Other clients stop and explain something else has to happen first, and still others may ask you to identify what is different from what has already been recorded. The clinician will want to explain the difference between processing thought and developing a plan of action by sharing the difference between thinking and doing (developing a plan).

Encourage

This component involves the development of a plan and corresponding timelines. By this time, the client's investment should be clear. If the plan is broad and does not have a timeline, there is a likelihood the client is not going to follow through. On the other hand, a strong, detailed, workable plan is likely to reflect the client's investment. This was the case with Leah's plan; the clarity and continuity of action from beginning to end suggest her personal investment in a plan to deal with difficult and unfamiliar challenges. She outlined changes in behavior with timelines for personal self-management. Of specific interest about Leah's response are the five noted timeline dates (today, today, we should know by next month, next month, two months), identified to monitor whether she and her boyfriend were going to have to take a different direction if the mother and mother's boyfriend choose not to pay any rent.

The entire activity concluded with Leah offering herself words of encouragement: We can do this! We have options to move forward! This suggests positive personal self-talk, tone, and level of optimism. Leah offered herself

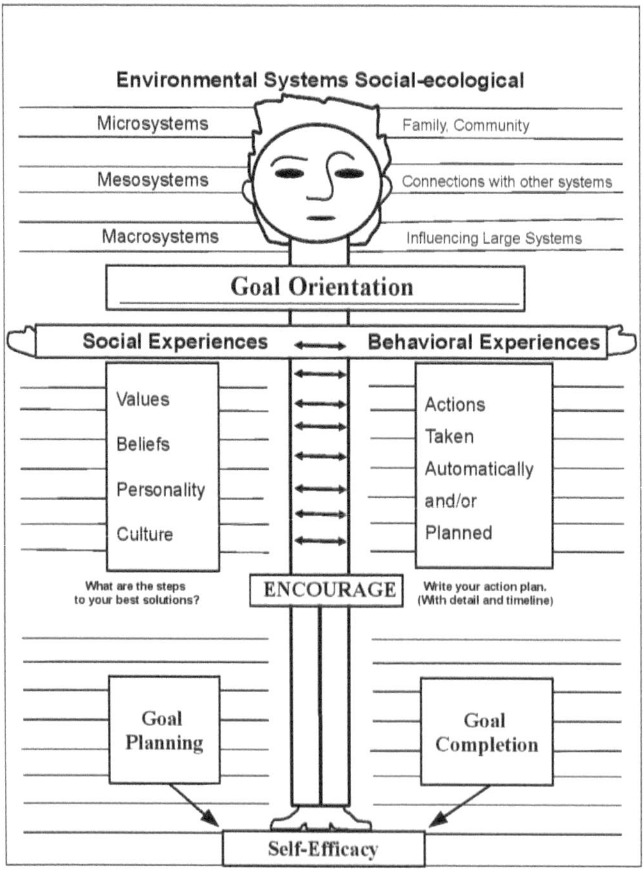

Figure 6.1 LIBRE Model with Categorical Data Elements

an encouraging phrase that may later prompt her to re-focus, self-regulate, and manage the challenge athand.

In sum, the data collected from the client suggests that Leah is someone who is self-aware (the detail provided about her social context), willing to invest in self (her detailed concern identified) and willing to explore change to resolve her identified challenge (the details of her plan and timeline).

Bandura[9] explains this internalized growth as a triadic reciprocal relationship involving the person's environment, self, and behavior. For example, a second career teacher will find this social cognitive learning is simultaneously communicated as experiences involving new environments, new self-roles, and new behaviors. The social cognitive triadic expression is complex; there are environmental changes from the exit of one profession and entry into a second, personal changes within the new classroom experience in relationship to prior first career experiences, and behavioral changes as the candidate considers past behaviors in response to new setting requisites.[10] Bandura[11] asserts that this phenomenon is a social force of self-change and development. For example, experiencing a novel environment will have an effect on behavior and self-management. Reciprocally, how one manages self and behavior will have an effect on how a new environment is viewed and processed.[12] Being able to manage problems, which arise, will further enhance functioning success during the transition period, leading to a place of well-being and positive emotions and views toward the future.[13] Without efficient skills such as problem-solving, transitioning into a new career may further compromise one's perceived competence and well-being. A high rate of self-efficacy will further lead to a sense of agency—that is, having persistence while experiencing challenging situations, thus leading to a proactive skill set in problem-solving engagement.[14]

Practice Client Exercise

Using the completed LMSFT worksheet completed in the prior chapter, analyze the data collected separating information by each of the five L-I-B-R-E prompts.

NOTES

1. Michelene T. H. Chi, Robert Glaser and M. J. Farr, eds., *The Nature of Expertise* (Hillsdale, NJ: Lawrence Erlbaum Associates, Inc, 1988); Gregory L. Murphy and Jack C. Wright, "Changes in Conceptual Structure with Expertise: Differences between Real-World Experts and Novices," *Journal of Experimental Psychology: Learning, Memory, and Cognition* 10, no. 1 (1984): 144–155.

2. Dale H. Schunk, "Goal Setting and Self-Efficacy during Self-Regulated Learning," *Educational Psychologist* 25, no. 1 (1990): 71–86.

3. Christopher M. Clark and Penelope L. Peterson, "Teachers' Thought Processes," in *Handbook of Research on Teaching*, 3rd ed., edited by Merlin C. Wittrock (New York: MacMillan Publishing Company, 1986): 255–296; Gaea Leinhardt and James G. Greeno, "The Cognitive Skill of Teaching," *Journal of Educational Psychology* 78, no. 2 (1986): 75–95.

4. Norma S. Guerra, "LIBRE Stick Figure Tool: Graphic Organizer," *Interventions in School and Clinic* 44, no. 4 (2009): 1–5.

5. Albert Bandura and Dale H. Schunk, "Cultivating Competence, Self-Efficacy, and Intrinsic Interest through Proximal Self-Motivation," *Journal of Personality and Social Psychology* 41, no. 3 (1981): 586–598.

6. Leon Festinger, *A Theory of Cognitive Dissonance* (Stanford, CA: Stanford University Press, 1957).

7. Fritz Heider, *The Psychology of Interpersonal Relations* (Hoboken, NJ: John Wiley & Sons Inc., 1958).

8. Edward L. Deci, Robert J. Vallerand, Luc G. Pelletier and Richard M. Ryan, "Motivation and Education: The Self-Determination Perspective," *Educational Psychologist* 26, nos. 3–4 (1991): 325–346.

9. Albert Bandura, "Social Cognitive Theory: An Agentic Perspective," *Annual Review of Psychology* 52 (2001): 1–26; Albert Bandura, "Toward a Psychology of Human Agency," *Perspectives on Psychological Science* 1, no. 2 (2006): 164–180.

10. Albert Bandura, *Social Foundations of Thought and Action: A Social Cognitive Theory* (Upper Saddle River, NJ: Pearson Education Prentice Hall, 1986); Albert Bandura, "Toward a Psychology of Human Agency," *Perspectives on Psychological Science* 1, no. 2 (2006): 164 –180.

11. Albert Bandura, "Social Cognitive Theory: An Agentic Perspective," *Annual Review of Psychology* 52 (2001): 1–26.

12. Bandura, "Social Cognitive Theory: An Agentic Perspective," 1–26; Albert Bandura, "Self-Regulation of Motivation and Action through Goal Systems," in *Cognitive Perspectives on Emotion and Motivation*, edited by Vernon Hamilton, Gordon H. Bower and Nico H. Frijda (New York: Kluwer Academic/Plenum Publishers, 1988): 37–61.

13. Amy L Reschly, E. S. Huebner, James J. Appleton and Susan Antaramian, "Engagement as Flourishing: The Contribution of Positive Emotions and Coping to Adolescents' Engagement at School and with Learning," *Psychology in the Schools* 45, no. 5 (2008): 419–431.

14. Patricia H. Miller, *Theories of Developmental Psychology*, 5th ed. (New York: Worth Publishers, 2011).

Chapter 7

Review of Collected Problem-Solving Units of Information

Engagement Styles

Competence is a combination of self-awareness and confidence to adapt rather than remain in past patterns.

Objective: To learn how to identify initial and sustained attention from the collected problem-solving units of information so that recognizable engagement styles can be incorporated for use within the intervention.

Engagement (attentiveness) is an important component of the counseling exchange. Risk is introduced when either the client or the clinician is not engaged. Yet this inherent simplistic concept is not often discussed, rather it is assumed. It is expected that the client and clinician are equally invested. But is this fact? This chapter addresses engagement styles as the observed combination of social cognitive and goal-setting data collected through the LIBRE Model problem-solving exchange. The chapter begins with a discussion of theoretical engagement, followed by the clinical problem-solving scoring and analysis of LIBRE Model data.[1] An engagement style rubric is presented, along with a step-by-step process for identifying client initial and sustained attention. We use the text client to illustrate how to score and analyze client responses. A discussion is presented on how to incorporate collected engagement data into the case plan, intervention, evaluation and resiliency development activity.

Theoretical Underpinning

Furrer and Skinner[2] define engagement as active, goal-directed, flexible, constructive, persistent and focused interaction with physical or social environments. Engagement addresses a personal style that is behaviorally observable and occurs within a social exchange. Counseling is one such social exchange.[3] Engagement is integral to one's sense of self: how one learns, how one attends and how one responds to the environment. The counseling session likely includes home, school, work and other larger contextual environments—all areas where engagement styles are observed.[4] Four engagement styles can be identified from a completed LIBRE Model exchange. As discussed in chapter 3 in reference to the service provider role, the open-handed, actual engagement parallels Furrer and Skinner's engagement definition. However, the problem-solving activity with its multiple foci cognitive components allows for the identification of variations to the actual engagement.[5] These engagement attentiveness preferences are observed when defining a problem, analyzing, evaluating and developing a resolution to provide the basis to the initial and sustained attention engagement rubric.[6]

Bandura's[7] core properties have much to add to this discussion; he asserts that to understand individual development, we must consider adaptability, engagement, personal management and changing behavior. He explains intentionality as a strategy and plan development, acquired skills that are used to act. Bandura further states that no one is a passive participant of life. Hence when a client lacks intentionality as observed within the context of clinical problem-solving, this becomes an engagement style marker. As a clinician I will want to begin generating exercises to explore this lack of intentionality. Additionally, forethought involves the development of goals and anticipated outcomes to guide encouraged investment; when this behavior is absent in the problem-solving, this too becomes an engagement style marker. It may suggest the need for additional data. In terms of intervention, teaching goal management may become the skill of choice.

As mentioned earlier, intervention selection is facilitated through task analysis, which involves identifying the smaller steps that make-up the identified task. The task analysis provides an order and priority that can then be used to present the intervention. What skills need to be developed, taught and monitored before going forward to achieve the desired social cognitive change? Bandura addresses this as self-reactiveness, the self-regulated choices and actions that are necessary to develop appropriate identified skills. This introduces the opportunity to teach self-regulatory skills in applied settings.

Self-reflectiveness is defined as one's self-examination (or regulation) of personal thought and metacognitive capacity and is seen in the client's efficacy. For example, how the client thinks about self and the confidence to consider options. Self-regulation is a skill that can be taught in a meaningful context to facilitate the client learning. Concrete examples from life are one way to introduce this concept. This approach allows for meaningful adaptive change in behavior to occur with a context that is relevant to the client. This also provides engagement information.

Self-regulation, a learned behavior,[8] interfaces with engagement. Self-regulation is an important consideration when examining engagement because self-regulation contributes to self-efficacy, confidence and competence. Carver and Scheier[9] explain self-regulation as cyclical feedback loops of past performance interacting with current performance to enable self-congruence (being consistent with self). These feedback loops operate independent of what is taking place in the environment. Individuals operate in behavioral patterns that depend on perception resulting in behavioral (self) consistency. Self-regulation is based on what we know of self, along with what we know of culture, beliefs and values to regulate accordingly. Patel, Glaser, and Arocha[10] assert that increased levels of recognized competence are a result of increased internalized self-regulation. This suggests that competence is a combination of self-awareness and confidence to adapt rather than remain in past patterns.

In this analysis, we consider culture as a contributor to identity[11] and engagement style as a means of representing personalized values, mores and beliefs.[12] As individuals develop, self-efficacy increases. Individuals raised in closed cultural systems may be challenged by social exchanges outside the familiar. When conflict occurs, behavioral responses are often distorted: overreacting, shutting down or some combination thereof. Maslow[13] explains that self-identity requires meeting hierarchical needs. Individual success is linked to managing and meeting needs to ultimately achieve self-actualization. Engagement styles drawn from the environment are influenced by context but not determined by it because sustainability is an element of engagement. The nature of successful engagement styles involves self-awareness and regulation, so attention switching can be taught as a self-regulated social cognitive monitor toward personal and professional success.

Clinical Problem-Solving Units of Information

This clinical relationship is ideal for a congruent client and clinician as long as each is ready to assume a problem-solving role. Accordingly, the client has freedom of expression, along with an opportunity to identify challenge and need. Meanwhile, the clinician observes the client's approach, processing and attentiveness to the defined problem. This context allows the clinician to analyze the client's entry to the problem-solving activity. The mid-thought processing involves the concern and thoughts associated with the concern. The process closes with the client resolution. As Bandura explains, we are not onlookers of life, nor are we products of behavior.[14] We interact and contribute, influenced but not without the freedom to adjust. Within the LIBRE Model problem-solving exchange, initial and sustained attention provide marked evidence thus creating engagement styles. Recording the client's actions in response to a self-defined challenge provides a wealth of information.

Engagement Styles

Engagement styles are personalized comfort zones for receiving, interacting and processing social contextualized environmental information.[15] Defined as the combination of initial and sustained attention and assessed with the LIBRE Model, two functions are provided by engagement style identification: (1) providing the client with an identified pattern for resolving conflict and (2) identifying the client's personalized mode in resolving self-identified challenges. The LIBRE Model responses are divided into two groupings. Initial attention is the combination of the L—listen, B—brainstorm, and R—reality-testing subset tasks. Sustained attention is assessed from the subset tasks of I—identify a concern and E—engagement steps, which include the development of a plan and the timelines for completion.

In addressing engagement styles, it is important to acknowledge that all of us, clients and clinicians alike, reflect a combination of learned and conditioned behaviors as we interact in social environments. For this reason, context must be considered in providing mental health services. In addition, client expressions (identified by the LIBRE Model) represent preferred means for receiving and filtering value systems, support systems and challenges. This is without regard to the individual's self-awareness. Finally, similar to Corno's[16] defined self-regulation, the LIBRE Model exchange involves volition, planning, metacognitive strategies and the willingness to be purposeful and staying focused to achieve the identified goal.

Initial attention is identified through the client's opening communication. It is the observed filtering or attentive detailed client expressions that are provided in response to the introduction to the problem-solving:

L: listen and list prompt as you ask the client to address what is occurring within the social environment,
B: brainstorming options, and
R: reality-testing possible implications.[17]

Initial attention is the first level of communication data marker. Behaviors, thoughts and contexts are processed in consonance with the client's willingness to be open and regulate attention or to present a closed, filtered expression. Is the client self-aware? Is the client attending to the interactive problem-solving dialogue? What prompts does the client act upon behaviorally with interest or not? Are the responses to the prompt confirmed through the language used? This initial communication sets the stage for client analysis; as a clinician, you want to monitor the client's words and behaviors. Make sure your client is comfortable with you; match your pace of speech to your client's pace. As the external person to the process, your goal is to observe and record your client-in-process. You do not want to be an intruder; you want to follow the client's lead in pace and volume so that as you analyze this data, it has been collected under the most ideal setting possible. This way you will attend to the details in measuring the client investment.

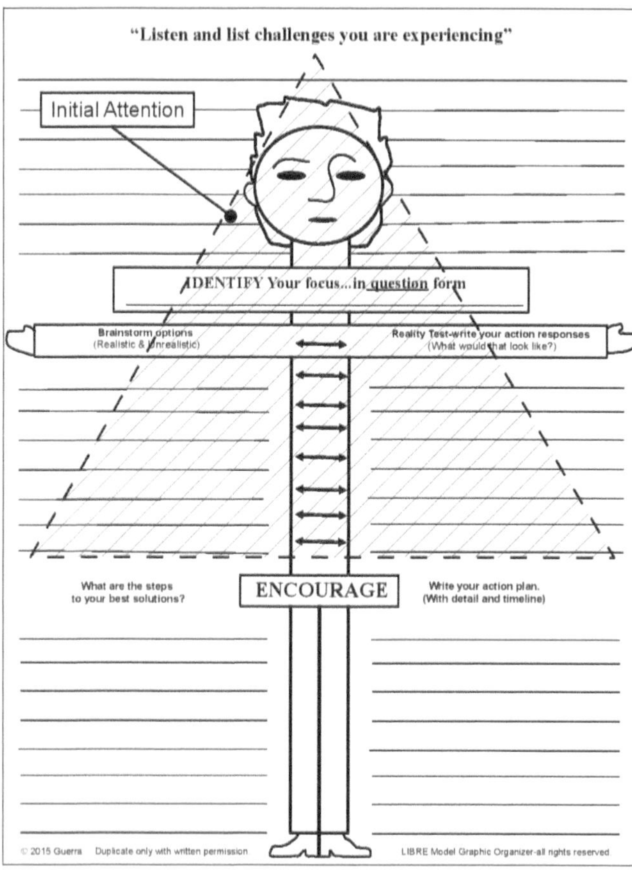

Figure 7.1 LIBRE Model Initial Attention

Sustained attention is identified through the client's maintained attentiveness to the LIBRE prompts:

I: identify a specific concern or goal and
E: encourage, which includes the development of a resolution plan and associated timelines.[18]

Sustained communication is an active or inactive investment in the problem-solving communication. As with initial attention, behaviors, thoughts and contexts are processed in consonance with a person's willingness and ease to manage and regulate a continued attentive communication. Watch closely for cues. For example, if the client begins to repeat herself, this is a data marker that her attention is waning. Conversely, if the client begins to exhibit increased expressed detail, this is a marker that indicates increased attentiveness. The largest data marker will be observed with the level of attentiveness to the client's resolution plan and timelines for completion.

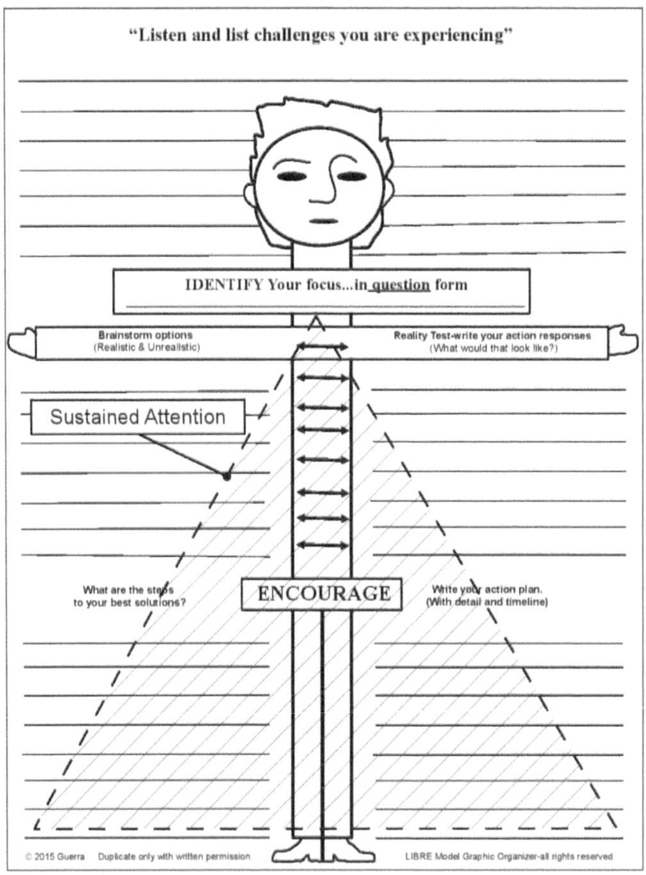

Figure 7.2 LIBRE Model Sustained Attention

Four engagement styles have been consistently identified in clinical studies.[19] Presented as quadrants, the styles include Actual Engagement, Potential Engagement, Goal-Focused, and Venting Engagement. The positive (+) and negative (–) signs represent participant investment and their placement represents attention, with the first sign indicating initial attention and the second signifying sustained attention.

Table 7.1 Engagement Style Investment

(+ high or – low) Initial Attention (Observable within the L–B–R responses) *(+ high or – low) Sustained Attention (Observable within the I and E responses)*	
Venting (initial investment, no commitment to plan or implement a plan) (+)/(–)	Goal-focused (limited initial investment, investment to a solution and plan) (–)/(+)
Potential (no initial investment, no sustained investment or commitment to a plan) (–)/(–)	Actual (initial investment, sustained investment and willingness to develop a plan) (+)/(+)

1. Actual Engagement Style. The client is open and relaxed, observed as cooperative and invested in terms of behavior, cognition, culture, and the social exchange. The client remains invested, offering new and additional details to each prompt up to and through to the close of the activity. This is observed as a realistic and detailed plan of action for the resolution of the identified challenge. Actual engagement style has a personalized script of (+ initial attention)/ (+ sustained attention).
2. Potential Engagement Style. The client is closed (filtered), using general (nonspecific) language, often repeating the same thoughts. Observed client behavior and dialogue appears more compliant as opposed to self-invested. The inactive client's tone remains consistent from the beginning to the close of the activity; the identified plan is vague, abstract, and nondescript. This personalized script is (–)/(–).
3. Goal-Focused Engagement Style. This client begins the session much like the potential engaged client, closed and not invested; however, once a personalized goal is identified, the self-regulated investment becomes visible as the client changes, becoming motivated. The client is focused, intentional, and almost effortless in developing a specific workable plan. This personalized style is scripted as (–)/(+).
4. Venting Engagement Style. Client is talkative, attentive, and ready to tell the service provider the narrative of life, problems, current affairs, etc. This initial investment may lead the clinician to think that the client is actually engaged; however, in listening closely, it becomes apparent that there is minimal to no interest in acting on any of the identified challenges. By the close of the session, no action plans are generated. The client is happy and may be most appreciative of the dialogue but with no interest in creating a plan. In some cases, the client frames all the problems with

variables outside his or her control; therefore, there is no value in attempting to generate a plan. This personalized style is scripted as (+)/(–).

Accordingly, engagement styles are assessed in how the client enters into, processes, and completes the LIBRE Model problem-solving activity. Like any activity involving multiple sub-skills and requiring continued attention, this metacognitive exchange is ideal for identifying engagement style even as you are beginning to know your client. You do not need to spend a great deal of time establishing the counseling relationship. Nonetheless, you should not assume that the client would come to each session with the same engagement style. Monitoring your client's engagement style is as important as the monitor of your own. What you want to observe is the consistency of a preferred engagement style in relation to an external social cognitive need and how the client adjusts. You want your client to learn additional efficient engagement styles along with becoming more self-regulated so that personal adjustments can be made to facilitate social exchanges. The engagement style information facilitates case plan generation and intervention development. Incorporating the content data with the processing engagement data will assist with a more complete intervention and opportunity to teach additional social cognitive and behavioral skills.

Assessing Engagement Styles

There are several steps to defining the client's engagement style. We first begin with the LIBRE Model Worksheet. The steps are as follows:

1. Conduct a general scan and assign numeric values of one or one-half point according to the type of information provided.
2. Each new or specific thought is assigned one point.
3. Repeated or general thoughts within the same prompt-category are assigned one-half point (see LIBRE Model Worksheet). For example, counting the number of listed items within the L—Listen and List challenges prompt, we would assign one point for each thought.
4. Once points are assigned, there is a second self-check to review your point allocations before proceeding. Using the Problem-Solving Engagement Style Prompt Cross-Checklist Worksheet, review your point assignment this time asking yourself: is this a specific item (1 point) or nonspecific or repeated item (.5 point). Read the content of your analysis and finalize the point assignments. This same scoring criteria and procedure is used for all LIBRE Model prompts with the exception of the I—Identify your focus cue. This item is scored either as one point when a single item is

entered that is within the client's control or one-half point when the topic or focus item is outside the person's control or a compound question. For example, how am I going to get my mother and Grandma to get along with each other?

5. We work with mean or average scores that are recorded as numeric counts for the two groups: initial attention and sustained attention (refer to the Problem-Solving Engagement Style Prompt Cross-Checklist and LIBRE Model Scoring Worksheet). We now enter the assigned values and calculate mean scores for each group. Let's walk through the scoring together using our text client, Leah, to illustrate.

Compare the expressed attentiveness with the Triangle I responses to those of Triangle II. If you have questions about your client's initial or sustained attention given the information provided (e.g., falls within the middle 3–4 range), identify all possible engagement styles and use that collected data to develop further inquiry. Follow-up data and problem-solving exchange responses with assist in identifying preferred engagement styles.

Step 1: using the LIBRE Model Scoring Worksheet, assign 1 point for each specific item and .5 point for a nonspecific or repeated item. Leah has eight items listed, so our first inclination would be to assign one point for each; however, pause here to review the Problem-Solving Engagement Style Prompt Cross-Checklist. After the second review, we see there are only seven specific items listed and one nonspecific item: there is a lot going on. We assign .5 point for the nonspecific item. We now enter 7.5 points onto the LIBRE Model Scoring Worksheet on the line reading Item 1.

Table 7.2 Problem-Solving Engagement Style Prompt Cross-Checklist

	Responses include: persons(s), place(s), things(s); counted & measured according to distinction & detail	
LIBRE Model prompt	*Specific items*	*Non-specific and/or repeated items with no new or additional information provided*
Listen & List	1 point	.5 point
Identify (focused concern)	1 point	.5 point if the question is general, outside the person's control and/or is a compound question
Brainstorm	1 point	.5 point
Reality-test	1 point	.5 point
Encourage (plan)	1 point	.5 point
Encourage (Timeline)	1 point*	.5 point

Table 7.3 Initial & Sustained Attention Scoring

Count of 5–8 investment	Count of 3–4 some investment	Count of 1–2 filtered or no investment
	Triangle I: Initial Attention	
Expressed self-awareness and social contextual connection	Minimum investment or filtered social connection	Filtered, minimal, or no initial investment
	Triangle II: Sustained Attention	
Focused self-awareness & willingness to explore change within one's control	Limited focus, diffused processing, may be a compound or broad question	Range of limited to no investment
Expressed commitment to explore and develop a plan	Some Commitment to develop a plan of action	Focused awareness of stressor, willingness to consider a plan

We go forward with the second prompt, I: identify your focus. Leah presents a challenge as a single focus and within her control. One point is assigned.

B: Brainstorm is assigned a total of 5 points; each is a unique thought, so each is counted. It does not matter that the client selected to delete them before moving to the reality-testing. We move to the second review using the Problem-Solving Engagement Style Prompt Cross-Checklist to confirm our point assignment addressing the specificity question.

R: Reality-test is assigned one point because Leah only carried over one option. We move to the second review using the Problem-Solving Engagement Style Prompt Cross-Checklist to confirm our point assignment addressing the specificity question.

E: Encourage steps to your best solution plan has 3 points assigned. We move to the second review using the Problem-Solving Engagement Style Prompt Cross-Checklist to confirm our point assignment addressing the specificity question.

E: Encourage timeline is awarded 5 points. We move to the second review using the Problem-Solving Engagement Style Prompt Cross-Checklist to confirm our point assignment addressing the specificity question.

Step 2: Review the assigned scores using the cross-checklist one final time, and make any final point assignment adjustments.

Step 3: Enter the values on the appropriate lines.

Step 4: Re-write the assigned values within the Initial Attention and Sustained Attention categories. Round up rather than carrying the fraction.

Step 5: Divide the Initial Attention group by 3 and place that value in the summary. Leah had a 7.5 for the L prompt; 5 for B prompt; and 1 for the R prompt for a total of 13.5 points. Divided by 3, her Initial Attention was 4.5, rounded up to 5 points.

Divide the Sustained Attention group by 2, and place that value in the summary section. Round up rather than carrying the fraction. Leah had 1 point for the I prompt, 3 points for the E prompt, and 5 points for the timeline. Divided by 2, Leah had a Sustained Attention of 4.5, rounded up to 5 points.

A general guide is provided at the bottom of the LIBRE Model Scoring Worksheet. As before, you will want to refer to the Problem-Solving Engagement Style Prompt Cross-Checklist to confirm your analysis. This is a data analysis of the client's words and observed expression. You are looking for patterns of initial and sustained attention. In Leah's case, she had an actual engagement style. The combined patterns are assigned one of the four engagement styles.

Below is Leah's scored worksheet. Each of the item numbers corresponds to the listings that were counted. Item 1. Is a count of the List prompt; Item 2. Identify your focus; Item 3. Brainstorm; Item 4. Reality-test and Items 6 and 7 are Encourage. Given the clinical nature of the contact, your scoring will reflect all client recorded data.

Integrated Initial Attention/Sustained Attention = Engagement Style

A sum of 3 or more is considered high while a sum of less than 3 is considered low.

- Venting Engagement Style: (High Mean Score)/(Low Mean Score) with no plan included.
- Actual Engagement Style: (High Mean Score)/(High Mean Score) with detailed plan with detailed timelines.
- Potential Engagement Style: (Low Mean Score)/(Low Mean Score) with the presence of a weak plan; that is general (not specific). Participant may report that they are already doing what they write out as the plan.
- Goal-Focused Engagement Style: (Low Mean Score)/(High Mean Score) with a greater focus on sustained attention rather than initial attention; the plan will include detail in steps and timeline.

Rationale for the Scoring Design

We address attention patterns to identify engagement styles. As we shift to analyzing the data, our examination is to the client's expressed attentiveness

List Challenges: Item 1__7.5__

Identify the Problem: Item 2__1__

Brainstorm Options: Item 3__5__

Reality Test Options: Item 4__1__

Encourage: (Planned Solution) Item 5__3__

Encourage: (Rehearsal) Item 6__5__

Sum of Item 1__7.5__

Item 3__5__

Item 4__1__

Initial Attention

Total__13.5__
Total divided by 3 = __4.5 » 5__

Sustained Attention

Sum of Item 2__1__

Item 5__3__

Item 6 __5__

Total__9__
Total divided by 2 = __4.5 » 5__

Summary:

Initial Attention __5__

Sustained Attention__5__

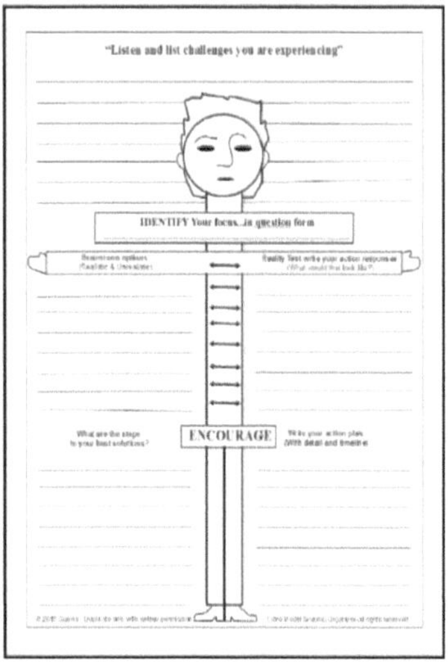

Figure 7.3 Scored Engagement Style Worksheet

to the self-defined problem. The data is analyzed by the detail expressed in association with the problem along with how the problem is framed (within or outside their control). With the model operating like a skeleton, we move our analysis from the bones (prompts) to the muscle (client response) of the exchange to identify the client's unique attentiveness patterns as revealed by their words and expressions. This is a clinical analysis; you are analyzing the client's snapshot taken by your LIBRE Model camera. Rather than focusing on each prompt, we examine clusters that represent initial and sustained attention. We use mean scores to provide an averaged value for initial attention. Sustained attention is slightly adjusted because the maximum value is one point assigned to the I—identify a focus prompt. With this one prompt response, it holds less value. The reason is linked to the problem-solving task and goal-orientation theory. If a goal is complex or outside my control, there is a greater likelihood that it will not be pursued. With the two attention averages, we look for highs (+) and lows (–), making our engagement determination from there.

Engagement Style with Content Data Added to Case Plan

The initial case plan is generated from the referral and client problem-solving content collected (how and what is defined as the problem). Together, the identified engagement style addresses the client's attentiveness and processing preference as viewed within the problem-solving task. You are now able to integrate the client's critical content and values expressed by the client's problem-solving experience and attentiveness-investment orientation.

In Leah's case, her expressed values focused on school, pregnancy and her current living situation. This information allows the clinician insight to better communicate within the client's ZPD,[20] describing the individual's personal problem-solving limits as an outline for potential growth. The clinician may also find that the client's ZPD is mediated by the identified engagement style, thus becoming an additional consideration for subsequent sessions.

While the focus in identifying a client's engagement style is not intended to change the clients' attention preference, it is presented to encourage the freedom to learn new strategies of self-management so the client can consciously switch from one engagement style to another. According to clinical observations, clients will often experience change in engagement style in response to mediating environmental stress or demands.[21] Counseling interventions involve the use of contextual matching and strategic mirroring to facilitate client response to environmental expectations. You want to be able to work with your client in the self-regulated engagement behaviors that will facilitate client gains.

Questions, Considerations, and Next Steps

As with any clinical analysis of client data, there may be either gray areas or non-dominate patterns introduced. Should this occur, record the suspected engagement styles and why you believe the client is not demonstrating one specific style. For example, if you believe your client is an actual engaged style but with some possibility that he is venting, by following up to explore whether the plan was accomplished, you will be able to confirm the engagement style. A venting engagement will not have a follow-up plan involving change. Continuing to collect data, you will be able to examine client preference in identified engagement styles. Once you have received sufficient data about the client's attentiveness and willingness to explore resolution change, this information can be added into your CMA intervention along with your generated notes.

Practice Client Exercise

Using the client's problem-solving data collected in practicing to administer the LIBRE Model in chapter 6. Score and incorporate the engagement style information into your practice case plan.

NOTES

1. Norma S. Guerra, "LIBRE Model: Engagement Styles in Counseling." *Journal of Employment Counseling* 44 (2007): 2–10.
2. Carrie Furrer and Ellen Skinner, "Sense of Relatedness as a Factor in Children's Academic Engagement and Performance," *Journal of Educational Psychology* 95, no. 1 (2003): 148–162.
3. Norma S. Guerra, "Illustrations of Engagement Styles: Four Teacher Candidates," *Teacher Education and Practice* 22, no. 1 (2009): 95–117.
4. Norma S. Guerra, "The LIBRE Model: A Cognitive One-On-One Loci Approach to Facilitating Change," (Paper presented at the Fall Teacher Education Conference, Waves of Change Consortium of State Organizations for Texas Teacher Education, Galveston, TX, 2004).
5. John R. Anderson, "Problem Solving and Learning," *American Psychologist* 48, no. 1 (1993): 35–44; Michelene T. H. Chi, Robert Glaser and M. J. Farr, eds., *The Nature of Expertise* (Hillsdale, NJ: Lawrence Erlbaum Associates, Inc, 1988).
6. Norma S. Guerra, "LIBRE Model: Engagement Styles in Counseling," 2–10.
7. Albert Bandura, "Toward a Psychology of Human Agency," *Perspectives on Psychological Science* 1, no. 2 (2006): 164–180.
8. Barry J. Zimmerman and Dale H. Schunk, eds., *Self-Regulated Learning and Academic Achievement: Theoretical Perspectives*, 2nd ed. (Mahwah, NJ: Lawrence Erlbaum Associates Publishers, 2001).
9. Charles S. Carver and Michael F. Scheier, "On the Structure of Behavioral Self-Regulation," in *Handbook of Self-Regulation*, edited by Monique Boekaerts, Paul R. Pintrich and Moshe Zeidner (San Diego: Academic Press, 2000): 41–84.
10. Vimla L. Patel, Robert Glaser and Jose F. Arocha, "Cognition and Expertise: Acquisition of Medical Competence," *Clinical and Investigative Medicine* 23, no. 4 (2000): 256–260.
11. Belinda Bustos Flores, Ellen Riojas Clark, Norma S. Guerra and Serafin V. Sánchez. "Acculturation among Latino Bilingual Education Teacher Candidates: Implications for Teacher Preparation Institutions." *Journal of Latinos and Education* 7, no. 4 (2008): 288–304.
12. Norma S. Guerra, Belinda B. Flores and Lorena Claeys, "A Case Study of an Induction Year Teacher's Problem solving Using the LIBRE Model," *New Horizons in Education, Journal of Education* 57, no. 1 (2009): 43–57.
13. Abraham H. Maslow, *Maslow on Management* (New York: Wiley, 1998).
14. Albert Bandura, "Toward a Psychology of Human Agency," 164–180.

15. Norma S. Guerra, "Illustrations of Engagement Styles: Four Teacher Candidates," 95–117.
16. Lyn Corno, "The Metacognitive Control Components of Self-Regulated Learning," *Contemporary Educational Psychology* 11, no. 4 (1986): 333–346.
17. Norma S. Guerra, "Illustrations of Engagement Styles: Four Teacher Candidates," 95–117.
18. Norma S. Guerra, "Illustrations of Engagement Styles: Four Teacher Candidates," 95–117.
19. Norma S. Guerra, "LIBRE Model: Engagement Styles in Counseling," 2–10.
20. Lev S. Vygotsky, *Mind in Society: The Development of Higher Psychological Processes* (Cambridge: Harvard University Press, 1978).
21. Maritza Lebrón-Striker, Personal Communication, August 1, 2006

Chapter 8

Intervention

Client Growth and Development

Self-regulated feedback is a powerful learning tool.

Objective: To examine the advantages of incorporating growth and social cognitive development client data into the Case Management Approach (CMA) intervention.

This social cognitive human growth and development presentation addresses two counseling states, first client growth—life-span essentials to engage clients in authentic communication toward change (where the client is within life) and second, client development—life-span self-regulatory interventions designed to promote personal growth and healthy positive self-regulated development (where they are in sustained adaptability toward lasting intervention impact). Erikson's theory of psychosocial development[1] is integrated with Bandura's[2] social cognitive learning theory to structure the client interaction and intervention. Erikson's theory of human development was selected to frame the human development presentation given its life-span extensiveness, social cultural orientation, and focus on identity development. Erikson's eight stages of human development[3] have been clustered into five groups (omitting birth to one year) based on differentiating social cognitive demands with respect to social environments: children to pubescent, adolescents, young adults, middle adults, and late adults. The five human development clusters are presented with suggested client growth cues, strategies, and activities to assist in engaging the client. Client development interventions consider social cognitive self-regulated skills toward positive change.

The goal of this chapter is to integrate Erikson's psychosocial ego stage development with Bandura's human experience—influenced by environment, mediated goals and with self-regulated plans—creates a climate for action. The two theoretical models are placed side-by-side to demonstrate how each facilitates a better understanding of the clients' growth and developmental strengths, challenges and opportunities. The chapter presents growth as the incoming counseling considerations that include: rapport, need identification as the case plan and the creation of an intervention plan. Development is presented as clinician considerations to nurture social cognitive adaptation techniques to engage the client, to introduce new skills, activity, and to address the intervention needs.

Client Growth

To provide significant client services, one must build a respected, engaged working relationship. Establishing a strong client-clinician bond begins with the clinician. The clinician's receipt of that initial referral and investment in understanding the client's 3Cs background (culture, cognition, and chronological age) is only the first step. Chronological age provides preliminary general information. To assess the client's background and social cognitive experiences, additional inquiry is required. Address where the client (client growth) is so that the intervention matches. This is the true working counseling relationship. You want your time and client's time to be invested in meaningful change. You may select to introduce one or more therapeutic techniques that will match the client and facilitate personal growth. The development is addressed as elements of the resiliency plan; the focus is on sustained acquired skills and behaviors.

Let's explore an example together. We will begin with an example involving a child then move to an example involving an adolescent, then a young adult and following each grouping with first growth (to establish rapport and begin teaching new skills) followed by development (to ensure the skills are learned and sustained).

As indicated within the referral, we have been assigned a five-year-old client who has been identified as being cognitively skilled and verbally mature as compared to other clients of the same age. We ask how we can prepare for the associated social cognitive development subtleties that may be encountered in working with this client. What do we need to consider to self-adjust to meet our client's differential needs? What type of developmental social (home, family, friends) and cognitive (formal and information learning) experiences should as we ready ourselves for our first meeting? A client human growth and development rubric has been created to examine each group. This listing includes suggested activities to engage the client and to understand the client's social cognitive experience. Interventions may also be created from this listing.

Child Growth

Beginning with the young child, two to twelve years of age, we return to our young client example; we know theoretically from Bronfenbrenner[4] that most young children have maintained primarily social cognitive exchanges involving family and home, but what is yet to be determined is how diverse these experiences have been within the family. Our strategy is to assume that the client has had concrete social cognitive experiences. An activity to initially engage the child may be coloring. While he colors, we will ask more abstract questions to examine parameters of thought (how the client responds and the type of language used). For instance, what is your favorite toy? How is your day going? Present a series of concrete open-ended questions that could then be followed by an exploratory, more abstract question about what he plans to do the next time there is a school holiday. Clay can also be used as a more abstract activity while addressing a concrete or abstract question. Socratic questioning can be strategically used to ask about the child's (social cognitive) experiences. If we elect to use the LIBRE Model problem-solving activity, we will need to simplify the exchange by framing the question for the child and then structuring the process for him. Returning to the example, the client is a five-year-old male. According to the referral, he ends up in time-out every day during recess. The coach says he does not know how to obey instructions. The consequence for his misbehavior is straightforward. The child is not allowed to have free play. Introducing the LIBRE Model and adjusting it to be more concrete and developmentally directive, we ask what he could do so he would not have to go into time-out every day.

The child replies, *I could get a dog.*

The brainstorming dialogue continues. *What would the dog do?*

Bite the coach, the child quickly replies.

We continue by moving from brainstorming to reality testing with the child. *But when the coach finds out it was your dog, then you and your dog and I will all end up in time-out. What else could you do?*

I know. I could get a monkey.

What would the monkey do?

He would bite the coach.

OK, but once Coach finds out it is your monkey, then you, the dog, the monkey, and I will all be in time-out. What else could you do?

Here the five-year-old client finally pauses to consider yet another option, but this time one within his control. *I know. If I sit down each time Coach tells me to sit down, then I will not be placed in time-out.*

> *Really?* We reply as the clinician, to which he gave a quick nod. Together we develop a plan, which included each time the coach said for him to sit, he would sit.
>
> The following day when he was asked about school, he was excited to report, I did not have to go into time-out, not one time.

This contextualized activity introduced an immediate solution, intervention, and behavioral change that resulted in his assuming personal control. It was a powerful lesson introduced in a timely manner to address an immediate problem.

Child Development

It is at this point as we continue to work with the clients, we want for them to invest in their personal growth toward healthy self-regulated lives. The development extends beyond the growth initially offered. Similar to strategy and activity adjustments made to engage the younger individual, there are intervening approaches to consider in matching clients' need. Play works well with children as an intervention to introduce new concepts. Questions about work or responsibilities provide you contextual information about the child's daily life that can then be used to create self-regulated interventions. With the five-year-old client, the follow-up inquiry is to see how he is monitoring his self-constructed plan. This exchange and additional problem-solving will help him begin to build a strong decision-making self-efficacy that facilitates future decisions.

The development phase involves the new change and new behaviors. We want to make sure that the child is able to sustain the developed new skills. It is at this point that information from the client interaction is noted in the development of the resiliency plan. Before we leave this child and his newly acquired skill, we want to make sure that his environment is able to assist the sustained change that has been introduced. For this small child, he now has a plan. Within our child development resiliency plan, we want to make sure that he is supported. Let's now look at adolescent growth and development.

Adolescent Growth

With adolescent clients, begin with a combination of concrete and abstract language as elements of your strategy. This might include questions about today's plans, future plans, and how the client describes self. The Socratic questions will facilitate your identification of social cognitive experiences. Should you determine the client is more concrete (by asking concrete questions) adjust to that language and continue with activities that are in line with the client's expressed preference. Hands-on activity will facilitate this initial engagement.

Examples include: Scrabble, hangman, or card games. As we speak with the adolescent and find that the client is more abstract in language and thoughts, then adapt your approach to use activities to facilitate continued engagement. For example, should the adolescent want to go to college, we might consider bringing a college application that could be completed as an activity. This type of activity will allow us to see how the client approaches the task, processes the questions, as well as how he or she describes self. Activities that require clients to describe self allow you to see how the clients' express and define themselves and identify development. LIBRE Model problem-solving may also work well as an initial activity. The client is free to define the problem and the immediacy of developing a resolution provides an outlet (if the client selects to develop a plan). Should a new skill need to be identified, narratives and role-play can be used to practice so the client becomes comfortable with the processing and execution of the new skill. Leah provides us an example of an adolescent. We incorporated the LIBRE Model problem-solving to begin working with her and to identify how she processed decisions.

Adolescent Development

Continuing with Leah to illustrate, hands-on activities work. Adolescents generally respond well to role-play. Practice social exchanges so that the new behaviors begin to feel comfortable to the client. It is quite common to see adolescents struggle with social exchanges, so interventions that include realistic experiences they may encounter will assist with the development of self-regulated skills. An adolescent who is angry because he does not believe his teacher is helping him provide an ideal opportunity. As the clinician and adolescent reverse roles so the adolescent is the teacher, he may assume a new appreciation for managing multiple requests at the same time. He can then be taught how to better ask for assistance. Once the behavior is practiced, the adolescent may likely report feeling empowered with his new skill. Self-efficacy and self-regulation are introduced with this type of contextualized intervention. The development plan is designed to support and sustain newly acquired skills. This information will also be incorporated into the resiliency plan.

As we revisit our text client Leah, she is struggling with a complex living situation that does not seem fair. Problem-solving has given her the opportunity for self-expression to voice her concerns. She was able to develop an intervention to her self-defined concern. As the clinician, you are able to process with her and allow her to practice the self-regulated steps. From this orientation, Leah begins to learn that no matter how complex a challenge may be, there is also an opportunity to self-manage according to one's values and beliefs—statements that you as the external clinician can make as observations. We had observed the growth that she has made but we also noted that sustaining that development will need external support. We will watch closely for how best to facilitate the maintenance of the newly acquired skills.

As we look at the young adult growth, new skills are introduced and development shifts our attention to how best to assist the client in sustaining those new adaptive changes. Rather than relying on external support, the young adults will be able to begin developing that network of support according to their own resiliency plan.

Young Adult Growth

Young adults should be approached from a more abstract perspective. We may want to consider a discussion about life goals, ambitions, and current or future relationships. Should we find that the client is agitated, we should adjust the dialogue using more concrete language and expression to engage the client. Matching our language (adapting our speech to be in line with the client) to that of the client's is always a subtle way of showing respect. For example, if the client has a pattern of pausing, we pause as we speak to the client or if the client says you know, we introduce you know into our communication. Start the conversation with the referral information received and with abstract-oriented questions. Come prepared with an activity that is more concrete until the client is relaxed as you approach the abstract inquiry. Activities may include cards at the concrete level (e.g., battle) or favorite magazines or journals at an abstract level. The LIBRE Model problem-solving activity works well with this developmental group because it invites self-expression from the content and language of choice. An example is Fred, a young man of 23 years. He is newly married, working and finalizing his undergraduate degree with aspirations of becoming a teacher. He is currently a student teacher; this is his final hurdle before graduation. He is however, running into a number of problems. Fred is requesting counseling because he was advised by his content master teacher and mentor that if he does not start arriving on time and ready to work, he will not be successful with his student teaching experience. You decide to problem solve with him. His goal is time management and he creates a detailed plan. You work together from setting-up a calendar to practicing how best to interact with his mentor and other student teachers.

Young Adult Development

Young adults work well with narrative scenarios in which they are able to problem solve or provide insight into identifiable challenges. Interventions should be pragmatically constructed. Returning to Fred, to sustain the changes that have been initiated, you might select to involve him in practicing new and developing skills that were introduced through an open-ended story designed to allow the client to process next steps. Intervention addressing unresolved issues or examining challenges from different perspectives facilitates self-regulation and self-awareness. For example, how he will make sure to arrive early and be prepared for each school day. Exploring complex interpersonal exchanges and practicing decision-making steps works well as intervention activities. Following up with a discussion of the client's processing can be used to encourage self-efficacy in processing complex issues. Thus once these skills have been acquired, you will want to make sure that they can be sustained. Ask the young adult what type of support would be needed for the newly acquired skills to be retained and internalized. Similarly, as we address the middle adult, growth to connect and development to sustain new skills will vary.

Middle Adult Growth

The middle adult should first be approached with a more abstract dialogue, using open-ended questions to explore language and social cognitive experience; include questions about aspirations, vacations, or hobbies. By this age, the individual has likely had a number of diverse social cognitive experiences. As we offer Socratic questions, listen closely to the client's language. As you are able to determine the client's concrete and abstract language and experience; shift yourself accordingly. Suggested activities may include card games. As both an activity and intervention, the LIBRE Model problem-solving allows clients to process a pressing concern and provide you information about their social cognitive experience. For example let's consider Lisa, a 45-year-old married woman with three children who cares for her in-laws. She reports being exhausted all the time and feels hopeless; her husband suggests she speak with someone so she has decided to come see you. After salutations and open-ended questions, you have decided to problem solve with her. Unfortunately, she is so overwhelmed by what is occurring in her life at this point, all she can do is state the problems and her brainstorming exhausts her. You encourage her with a positive word and explain that this is just a beginning point. You will work together with the agreed upon goal of her better organizing her thoughts and actions. Over the next several months a number of changes have occurred. You had recommended that she see her physician, she is now taking vitamin supplements and has joined a gym. Lisa has now realized the importance of self-care. She works with a schedule that includes time for her. These gains have provided Lisa with new energy.

Middle Adult Development

We will want to determine the client's engagement style and consider whether the engagement style contributed to the referring problem. For example, if the client has a venting engagement style and has been referred because the client never finishes what she starts, then we will likely find this same pattern demonstrated as the lack of sustained investment in how she completes the problem-solving activity. This allows us the opportunity to show the client in her own words how her investment has waned prior to completing this problem-solving task. Her own words are used to demonstrate the challenge. This allows us to teach how to set-up and manage a goal and becomes the intervention. Monitoring accountability to completing self-determined goals will facilitate increased self-regulation. The client's developing self-awareness becomes an important skill. Such was the case with Lisa. She was overwhelmed and was not able to complete the problem-solving activity. The venting was identified with the problem-solving and her inability to complete the activity. As time continued, she learned how to hold and sustain goals that began with her care for self and extended beyond in caring for her family and in-laws.

Intervention activities for the middle-age adult may include a variety of role-play, or instructional practices to keep the client engaged while addressing challenging social cognitive challenges. Using the LIBRE Model[5] and sharing patterns in responding to the problem-solving exchange can be quite eye opening. Many clients, after reviewing their problem-solving patterns, are surprised to realize that challenges can be self-generated and self-maintained. Thus, the intervention and monitoring of change are introduced within the naturalistic context. The client is invited to reflect on new skills introduced and learned. The client is less likely to be resistant when they see themselves partners in the development of the new positive adaptive change. For example, a client who has had only venting experience and when asked to problem-solving, his response is to vent. Once the pattern was realized, the client was able to see that the current approach was not facilitating. Goal setting was then embraced and became the intervention of choice. The client learned the new skill and became the self-regulator of the skill from an empowerment posture. Vygotsky's work with ZPD[6] shows the importance of scaffold assistance to learn and provide feedback to introduce self-reflective growth; the self-regulated feedback is a powerful learning tool. Ask your middle adult client about skill maintenance and develop a plan to sustain the new skills. This information will then be included in the resiliency plan as with the other groups.

Late Adult Growth

When working with late adults, begin with concrete language. For example, how is your day? Or, what did you do today? Consider activities that are simple and more hands-on, like drawing. Our goal is to engage the client. If we find that this person is more abstract, then adjust our language accordingly and consider activities that involve planning or the future. Match the client's pace and use language that is similar. Assume that our client has had a variety of social cognitive experiences; ask about a favorite job or hobby. Use the referral to invite the client to speak to his or her view of the presenting problem. Once you have connected with the late adult, you are ready to introduce your interventions. Monitor the skills developed. An example is Linda, an eighty-five-year-old woman who lives alone. Her son who believes she needs to talk to someone about this problem has referred her to counseling. After seeing Linda, you note that she does have some challenges in remembering, however, she also appears to be aware of this change and has already visited with her doctor. You decide to problem solve with her and she says that she is easily distracted. She develops a plan to help her focus but also tells you that she does not like to work with 'To-Do Lists. To make the activity more fun, you ask her if rather than words, would she like to organize her day with pictures. She laughs and says, I really like the idea and it sounds like fun; then, I can post my pictures to help me remember. She draws pictures to remember to turn off the lights, lock the doors, and turn off the stove. Months have passed and this seems to be working. Linda enjoys drawing and has decided to go to the community college to take a drawing class.

Late Adult Development

It is important to facilitate and match the client in language at this point more than at any other developmental point. Client-counselor boundaries are important. We do not want to overinvest, rescue, or the reverse—underinvest. Instead we will want to involve clients in change without distressing them. Human psychosocial ego[7] and social concerns set the stage for decision making, while human agency as influenced by environment mediates goals and self-regulated plans to decisions. As we consider interventions, work with more concrete tasks to facilitate learning. If the client, as was the case with Linda, is having difficulty remembering, we might want to explore with the client better ways to remember. We contextualized the intervention into an activity that will make the client comfortable. Drawing pictures to explore how pictures can be used to remember key information, or keeping notes gave her an empowered control. Her decision to take an art class addresses her continued development. Encourage client management and assist with self-regulation while introducing the importance of being open to external support or assistance. Of importance in your self-managed role is setting the stage for the initial engagement and necessary adjustments that may need to occur to assist clients with their development. Once those skilled are learned, create a development plan that addresses how best to sustain each of the acquired skills.

Table 8.1 Client Growth and Development: Social Cognitive Counseling Exchange

	Counseling Exchange Strategies	*Suggested Growth Activities*
Children	Use concrete language	Hands-on activities; practice play to build skills
Adolescents	Use a combination of concrete and abstract language	Practice social exchanges and role-play
Young Adults	Begin with language and adjust: Abstract > Concrete	Narrative and role-play
Middle Adults	Abstract > Concrete	Narrative and games
Late Adults	Abstract > Concrete	Hands-on

Clinician's Social Cognitive Adaptations

To summarize, the CMA partnership begins with the clinician's calibration. We have a primary role to be open, poised and flexible to adjust with each client. This self-check and engagement-regulated behavior facilitates the counseling exchange. This calibration implies the importance of change. We communicate to the client that we are encouraging, expecting and providing opportunities for client development through self-reflection. Thus, this self-check task is completed first. Our personal state of development is observable within this social contextual adjustment. As a social cognitive experience, the clinician is modeling self-regulated engagement for the client.

Socratic Questions

Mastering open-ended questions is one of our most powerful tools for assisting clients. Strategic questions that are presented within the flow of the working relationship will introduce the client to new thoughts and skill considerations. They may include questions about questions, questions to probe or lead or questions to stimulate further thought. The associated rationale is simple. Genuine interest and willingness to listen, opens the door to valued and shared communication. Open-ended questions look different at the distinct ages; you should prepare questions prior to working with any one group. Develop a question bank for the different groups so you are able to adjust from concrete to abstract or abstract to concrete. You will find that there is a large return in asking an open-ended question instead of telling someone what to do. Similarly, asking a closed-ended (give me the facts) question has a limited return.

Practice Exercise

Refer back to the administration of the LIBRE Model and incorporate the human development and social cognitive needs into a case conceptualization plan.

NOTES

1. Erik H. Erikson, *The Life Cycle Completed: A Review* (New York: W.W. Norton & Co, 1982).
2. Albert Bandura, "Toward a Psychology of Human Agency," *Perspectives on Psychological Science* 1, no. 2 (2006): 164–180.
3. Erik H. Erikson, *Childhood and Society* (2nd ed.) (New York: W.W. Norton, 1963).
4. Urie Bronfenbrenner, "Ecological Systems Theory," in *Annals of Child Development: Vol. 6. Six Theories of Child Development*, edited by Ross Vasta (Greenwich, CT: JAI Press, 1989): 187–249.
5. Norma S. Guerra, "LIBRE Model: Engagement Styles in Counseling," *Journal of Employment Counseling* 44 (2007): 2–10.
6. Lev S. Vygotsky, *Mind in Society: The Development of Higher Psychological Processes* (Cambridge: Harvard University Press, 1978).
7. Patricia H. Miller, *Theories of Developmental Psychology,* 5th ed. (New York: Worth Publishers, 2011).

Chapter 9

Intervention Evaluation

Managing Change and Crisis Situations

Change can produce behavioral, physiological, psychological, and social cognitive transformations, some of which are positive, others unwelcome, with most manifestations including gradients between the two extremes.

Objective: To develop a strategy and plan to assist with clients' changes and crises.

Change can produce behavioral, physiological, psychological and social cognitive transformations. Some of these manifestations are positive, others not however more common are the gradients of these two positive-negative extremes. While we tend to associate risk with extremes, there may also be risk with gradient levels of change. Thus, for the clinician monitoring change is a critical responsibility. The client is learning new skills, practicing new processes and likely receiving new reactions from those within the immediate social context. This phenomenon is referred to as Bandura's triarchic reciprocality in which the person interacts with environment, person-self, and behavior, even as each impacts the other. Therefore as clinicians, we should not assume that the clients' processing of change will be predictable.

Observational skills and Socratic questioning are critical. You are actively monitoring the client's behavior and feedback as you introduce the client to new social cognitive skills. You (with the client) may be the person who makes the initial call for help on behalf of your client. For example, you note visible acting-out behavior and anxiety that would suggest to you that something has happened to your client. On further inquiry, you identify that the client is experiencing depression and expressing at-risk behaviors. You shift your attention to collecting additional data. At this point, you may want to refer to any prior data collected and questions you may have created for yourself such as: What was the impetus for the change in behavior? Was there a trigger to this behavioral change? When did this change occur? How long has this behavior been in place? According to the CMA process, you will make the clinical judgment to report, refer, or seek medical assistance on behalf of your client. For those not working for an agency, it is important to have established parameters in your practice for when to report, what to report and to whom.

In this chapter, we discuss social cognitive changes associated with potential concern or crisis. Our examination of risk begins with the clinician's role. We then address the CMA client-framed data: context, culture, cognition, chronological age, and social cognitive human growth and development information along with the client's problem-solving and engagement. Next, we address options to consider in identifying and developing intervention strategies and use problem-solving as a monitoring tool to teach client self-managed approaches to mental wellness. Discussed in this chapter are safety plans, when to report and how to ensure safety for all involved.

Clinician Role

The mutual relationship shared between the client and clinician shifts in weight and responsibility as the clinician notes that the client exhibits a noted difficulty. While in session, the clinician always maintains a monitoring role. Once the client exhibits a troublesome affect to an intervention, the clinician will immediately shift to explore what is happening with the client. The communication begins with an open-ended question and observation of the client in response to the question. For example, I noticed that something has changed. Want to talk about it? If the client does not immediately speak, the clinician may select to address the changes that have been observed. This allows the client to self-reflect and, if willing or self-aware, express what is occurring. The CMA provides a tremendous advantage for you as the clinician at this point. The comprehensive data you have been tracking with each session now becomes your client-contextualized data from which to gauge any negative change that may be occurring. We use collected CMA data and format to review what that would look like for you as the clinician. Let's bring back our text client Leah to process potential risk.

Text Client Update

It has been one week since we last met with Leah. According to our CMA, we had only planned to see her three times. The first two sessions went well. This is now the third session and she comes into the session with a sadness that cannot be ignored. She has lost weight; she looks like she has not slept in days, and her clothes are wrinkled. We have never observed her in such an unkempt state.

As with each prior session, we begin with the established introductions. Noting the visible changes, we adjust our plan for the session. Rather than beginning with a review of last week's homework and the agenda for the session, we begin with an open-ended question.

> She quickly replies, *nothing is going to change with the apartment and my boyfriend. He told me he doesn't intend to do anything about it.* She continues with tears in her eyes. *My boyfriend says he loves his mother very much and he would never do anything that would hurt her. He told me that he is all she has.* She pauses. *As a matter of fact, he got so angry he told me if I didn't like it, maybe I should go home . . . it wasn't like I was paying rent either.*
>
> There is a long pause in her update, and as the clinician, we decide to let the silence continue.
>
> Leah composes herself and continues to cry softly, pausing only to wipe her eyes and nose as she speaks. *I don't know what I'm going to do.*
>
> *Is that something you would like to talk about?* We ask.
>
> *I don't know. I'm afraid to think this could be the end of our relationship.*
>
> *So where are you right now with your thinking?*
>
> *I think I need to go to the restroom. I'll be right back.*
>
> *Of course.*
>
> This becomes our moment to process Leah's change and this is our introduction to the client's managing change and crisis presentation.

Analyzing Base Data to Determine Risk

We use the CMA collected data as the foundation to this assessment. The very first step is to consider her social cognitive functioning ability. Because Leah's behavior, mood, and expressed cognitive functioning had been positive in prior sessions, this is a marked change. We immediately examine her social contextual information and additional questions generated over this three-week period; these are questions that have never been asked.

This ongoing development of questions is another advantage to the CMA because we have generated questions within each of the CMA sections. We begin with a review of our collected data according to the CMA record.

Contextualized Change

Section one of the CMA form data indicates that over the last two sessions, Leah has been willing to problem solve and it was noted that she was exhibiting an actual engagement with each of the prior sessions. These are questions developed within this area: How much of a preference does Leah have to an actual engagement? Does she ever shift from the observed and assessed actual engagement style?

Observationally, it does appear that Leah is at risk; she is exhibiting some stress. If she continues as an actual engaged client, we may expect that her investment in the relationship and the response from her boyfriend have affected her profoundly. We know that actual engaged individuals process with keen sensitivity from the beginning to the end; they experience the same intensity as they begin all the way to the close of the task at hand. We anticipate that she may be feeling out of control, seeing herself as not being effective in working with her relationship and her living situation. We note that she takes a moment to compose herself, which may be her attempt to shift herself away from actual engagement. Or she may just need a moment for herself with the expectation that she will remain actually engaged. We want to determine if she is acting from an actual engagement style to define level of risk to self, even as she prepares to address the challenge at hand. What we want her to explore here is what is going on with her right now: her feelings, thoughts, and state-of-being. We want her to understand that taking time to process slows everything down, allowing her time to think. And we want her to understand that thinking is as important as taking any action.

Referral

We review the referral, which indicates her grades are slipping because of her absenteeism. Questions generated here include: Because she is a minor, what happens if her parents are contacted because of her absenteeism? Who cares for the baby if she is going to continue going to school? Her parents are still responsible for her; at what point should the parents be contacted?

We are concerned that Leah does not identify her parents as a support. Her parents still have a legal responsibility to care for her. We will want to visit again with the teachers who introduced the referral to see if anything has changed and the parents who signed the initial referral for Leah to receive services. This will be our opportunity to collaborate and either confirm or negate our suspicions.

Culture

We now review our CMA notes to determine her current expressed cultural behavior in relation to her prior cultural expressions. Questions were developed; both those asked and not asked are evaluated. We note her stated cultural thoughts associated with moving outside her home. She has reported that this is consistent with her family values and belief systems. Leah had identified this as a natural next step. She was going to have a baby, so she expressed her need to begin a new life. She indicated that other family members had already left home to start a new life once they found out they were pregnant, so culturally this was an appropriate next step. This was expressed as a socially acceptable practice. The notes include a client quote made with the initial meeting: you fall in love with a person who is expected to be with you for life.

From our notes, we see that she expressed the decision to move in with her boyfriend. Family cultural background data suggests that this was an appropriate cultural and social decision. This decision is within her normal view of life. This has been confirmed by speaking with Leah's parents. These notes, however, allow us to generate additional questions about this current partner: what if this intended lifetime commitment is not a lifetime commitment for her or him? What if remaining with her boyfriend takes her outside her cultural competency? What will her family say if she wants to return home? Will her family let her return home? What if she decides to do something different from what her other family members have done? This leads to questions about what might happen if Leah decides to move into a shelter away from home and her boyfriend or if she stays in school and gives up the baby for adoption or terminates the pregnancy.

At this point, we have noted her conservative responses to each of the identified challenges presented thus far with the first and second problem-solving exchanges. We also note that she believed moving away was the culturally accepted behavior for where she is in life. We will want to explore her support system. What options does she see for herself? If she did decide to return home, what would this imply to her and to her family? Is that even a culturally acceptable consideration? More importantly, we want to ask her what she is considering and if she has a support system as we consider her future development.

Cognition

Prior to the pregnancy, Leah had been doing well in school. Her teachers report that she is a strong student. With this life change, her grades and attendance have changed. Questions here include the following: Do her teachers see any additional changes since Leah has been in counseling? Are her teachers aware of what is occurring outside of school? Has Leah been provided the opportunity to make-up her missing work? If so, has she been able to complete that work? What type of grades is she making on these assignments? Are there noted differences in how she is making decisions or problem-solving from the first to the second to this third session? We are also looking for cognitive changes in judgment as compared to prior decision plans she generated.

Chronological Age

Leah is still an adolescent. Questions generated (but not yet asked) include the following: What about her decision to live with her boyfriend? Is she starting to have regrets about her decision? If she wants to return home, will her parents allow her to?

Social Cognitive Human Development

Leah has expressed that she never had this type of interpersonal relationships before. This is her first boyfriend. And of course, she knows that he loves his mother; she loves her mother, too. She knows what it is to love your mother, but she has no context in how to judge his mother's boyfriend. She came from a traditional family structure with parents who have been married for years. This is very unfamiliar to her. While she is chronologically at an adolescent stage of development, according to her social context, she is addressing identity vs. identity diffusion issues. She is currently operating at a young adult level, struggling with intimacy and solidarity vs. isolation with little to no experience in how to proceed.

While Leah exhibited no distress during the two earlier sessions, at today's session, she does appear to be anguished. Therefore, our questions include these: How different is she in presentation and management as compared to her earlier sessions? How willing is she to continue processing the interpersonal relational exchanges? Is she remaining congruent with herself (and her development)? Is she more willing to remain with what is familiar to her or to continue to struggle with issues of intimacy and identity development?

Next steps in identifying and developing intervention strategies. At this point, we have identified some risk as contextualized using Leah's data. We have also determined six overarching categorical questions. We begin by summarizing and identifying these:

Engagement/Content: what is her engagement style in this moment? Is she willing to share her thoughts in problem-solving? Is her engagement style different from the earlier sessions?

Referral: we will follow up with referring teachers and parents to confirm the potential risk that we have identified. We will then target that specific change in behavior.

3Cs: Culture: we are interested in identifying culturally appropriate support. Does Leah have a support system? Is the support at school or outside of school? If outside school, is it family or her boyfriend? Does Leah have any close girlfriends? Are Leah's parents prepared to welcome her home?

Cognition: we want to explore her thinking. Have there been changes in her decision making? Is she making better decisions? Has she cognitively shutdown?

Chronological Age: as a minor, we must include the parents' responsibility for Leah's welfare. Will her parents allow her to return home? Do her parents acknowledge/accept any responsibility regarding Leah?

Social Cognitive Human Development: we review Leah's individualized environmental experiences. Will Leah return to her more familiar developmental stage, or will she continue to struggle with issues of intimacy and identity development?

Assessed Case Summary

We have decided that rather than asking all of the questions that have been generated, we will hone in on several key questions and observe her responses. We ask those select questions and watch closely for the nonverbal or indirect information provided. It is anticipated that this information will assist in providing sufficient information. Therefore, we will likely not return to the bank of generated questions.

We determine that closing this client contact as originally proposed is not appropriate. Instead, we will recommend that she continue to receive services. We also decide that the family should be contacted. However, given the six overarching questions, and the limited information we have about her support system, we resolve to continue using the problem-solving exchange with her. As an ongoing activity, we believe new goals should be introduced to best support herself. We select to assist her in establishing a support system, which is in keeping with the agency policy. We will visit with Leah about this plan and share the rationale for contacting her parents. We will also share what her parents will be told so she will be able to see herself as a participant in next-step decisions. We are now ready to begin this third session, just as Leah returns from the restroom. She appears to have combed her hair and washed her face. She has stopped crying and apologizes for having kept us waiting.

Problem-Solving as a Monitoring Tool

The utility of the LIBRE Model is in how it can be used. For Leah, re-introducing it at this point of crisis will assist on multiple levels:

1. We will be able to determine her engagement style, which will also allow us to introduce self-care.
2. We will be able to address her thoughts as she defines and processes what she is experiencing. We will be able to determine risk.
3. We are empowering her to speak for herself, to hear her own voice, and to reflect on her own thinking.

If there is a need for a more overt intervention, having this additional information will be important to the next-step actions or referrals.

Safety Plans

After visiting Leah, we did identify risk. We have also determined that it will be important to report; we will inform her of the decision and we will document challenges using her own words. While the risk does not appear to be life threatening, she is not prospering in her current setting. Our developed safety plan will be constructed with Leah and it will likely include her parents as the immediate contact. As much as possible, we define the plan according to what is realistic for the client.

Let's examine a different assessment of Leah. This time, let's assume that Leah indicates that her only option is to end her life. We will process this with her; we will ask about details in taking her life to establish the severity of the risk and with this information recorded in her own words, we will report.

Let's assume that the text client change went in a different direction. For example, let's say that Leah indicates that her boyfriend has beat her and that if she tries to leave him, he has indicated that he will kill her and her unborn baby. At one level, we assist her with developing a safety plan, which will include how to move to safety if he comes after her. And again, because she is a minor, we would report according to school and agency procedures and of course, notify her parents. It is obvious that the clinician actions will need to be timely. We will want to work within agency directives including the required notification to the police. It is likely that you as the clinician will be the person who will make this call.

How you determine to sequence these steps is up to you. Some agencies may have a protocol. It is always advisable to inform the client. Leah should be apprised of this next step.

Boundaries are created to support ethical responsibility and ethical decisions. When a client's safety is at hand, you will want to be forthright in not extending your boundaries; rather, hold to the identified protocol and as necessary, call the police. At the lowest level, your role is to cause no harm and if overextending an already at-risk client is a consideration, you will need to self-regulate accordingly. Even if Leah cries and begs you not to report, you have an ethical responsibility to report.

Practice Client Exercise

Lee has been your client for two weeks; you have seen him once. The human resources department has referred him to you. He was reported as anxious and depressed by his coworker, who contacted the boss. Lee has no listed family or support system. He has been wearing the same clothes to work for several days in a row. He reports having no energy and says he is too tired to care about dressing for work. You have been asked to assess personal risk and offer recommendations. List your assessment of risk and indicate recommendations you are willing to provide.

Chapter 10

Resiliency Plan

Developing Resiliency through Self-Regulation

Resilience includes not only adaptation but also all the opportunity to thrive even when negative events are experienced.

Objective: To examine the development of the client resiliency plan for continued personal growth and development in sustaining skills once counseling services end.

This chapter addresses resiliency with reference to work by Skinner and Pitzer;[1] Appleton, Christenson and Furlong;[2] and Fredricks, Blumenfield, and Paris,[3] along with others who have researched the value of teaching resiliency as an intervention strategy. Resiliency is presented in terms of engagement (an active motivational factor) and self-determination theory, which embraces the principle of meeting basic human needs. Our approach assumes that each person has needs that are met through social exchange therefore, persons engage. When needs are not met, behavioral manifestations occur. One such example is acting-out behavior.

The goal of this chapter is to provide you with resiliency constructs and continued client development resources that can be used with your clients. Resiliency must be established for client sustained success and culmination of the CMA. We will use resiliency and self-regulation skills to prepare your client for future independent decision making. The next step includes addressing the future—a strategy for nurturing sustained social cognitive development. Protective factors are discussed as resiliency strategies that incorporate social cognitive and goal-oriented problem-solving with self-regulation. By the end of this chapter, you will be able to use the client-contextualized CMP information in the development of criteria to customize protective factors to assist the client in maintaining achieved gains realized as a result of the time invested in counseling.

What is resiliency? The reality is that there is no one definition for resiliency or resilience. It is an acknowledged and researched construct that will continue to be studied into the future. Nonetheless, to facilitate our discussion and application, we begin with a general orientation; resiliency is the dynamic process encompassing positive adaption within the context of significant adversity.[4] Resilience includes not only adaptation but also all the opportunity to thrive even when negative events are experienced.[5] Resiliency is a specific form of personal agency that is influenced by ecological contexts.[6] Thus, there are many stories of individuals who have positively thrived rather than becoming victims of encountered challenge. Social cognition, goal orientation, and engagement (as self-regulation in awareness and motivation) describe and set the stage for our contextualized resiliency.

Resilience addresses an individual's adaptive response to experienced adversity. Let's illustrate: Two young boys were born and raised within the same community. Each was talented, skilled, and held goals and plans for himself. As they grew, both experienced challenges. The hardships were similar for each young man; however, one became bitter, cursing the darkness and moving away from his goals and dreams. The other selected a different path. He reflected; he thought that he must have missed a cue. He began to work harder to actively learn why and what he could have done differently from the experienced challenges. He wanted to learn from those experiences. He sought positive, supportive friends, and he used his talents and skills to become more successful in his thinking and planning. The result was adaption toward a successful outcome. The second young man was pleased as he reflected upon his success.

Three occurrences frame this story:

1. Equal starting points
2. Each boy had equal skills and talents
3. Adversity presented as challenge
4. Equal opportunity for behavioral adjustments.

Resilience was only evidenced in the second young man and his positive adaptations to adversity. This is where our discussion begins.

Skinner and Pitzer[7] assert that the study of engagement (as an active behavior) can be improved by introducing concepts of everyday resilience. They suggest value in allowing students to make mistakes to promote personal and interpersonal resources. Hardiness (another term used for resilience) is developed from falling down and being able to stand up again. It is also sometimes referred to as grit and described as perseverance. In terms of self-efficacy, there is a confidence that is learned from being able to overcome challenge.

The perceived belief in self will encourage individual persistence, to continue in the midst of adversity with the confidence that the goal will be achieved.

Academic engagement suggests the importance of proximal processes. Resilience is observed in perseverance, persistence, and processing of environmental encounters. It involved the individual interpreting these conditions as situations or events that can be overcome to achieve the desired goal. Bronfenbrenner and Morris[8] suggest that learning and adaptation occur in the midst of these interrelational social exchanges, thus resulting in cumulative and long-term change. They assert the importance of personal environmental event interpretations (that may be occurring within the individual's immediate experience and self-interpreted) to suggest that the person's view will create change.

Counseling impact is measured through positive sustainable change. To facilitate this mental health adaptive advantage, we want to consider clients' perceptions or personalized interpretations toward sustaining change. Our clients need to be able to see that they are able to self-manage their changes. Scaffold support so that they are able to go forward into their defined communities with the confidence that as challenge occurs, successful resolution can follow. Let's examine client-constructed resiliency as a response to the complexity of the client's social exchange. We begin with social cognitive change maintained through self-regulation, goal orientation, and managed within the clients' ecological (individual-within-community) interface.

Beginning with the familiar, academic mentors work with students to develop personal goals, problem-solving skills and the strategies to sustain a focus on self-determined, self-directed, and self-regulated learning. There is a wealth of research to support these approaches to help students develop independence as self-regulated learners.[9] Similarly, mental health providers work closely with their clients to acquire self-regulated independence through the integration of positive change. They assist clients in a supportive environment to learn how to monitor personal engagement, set goals and teach clients how to self-regulate their progress forward in reaching their goals. The problem-solving CMA is used to guide, monitor, and measure client change and investment. This same process can be used to assist with the development of resilience strategies. As Dillen[10] asserts, resiliency helps individuals proactively move into conditions to thrive. Therefore, to be able to assist someone, we must collect sufficient information to determine potential challenges from the environment. Similarly, client vulnerabilities (from prior reactions and behaviors exhibited) must be identified. The more data and social cognitive contextual information collected, the clearer the best/appropriate resilience plan will become.

Ecological pictures can be used to examine contexts because they will provide a client's personalized picture of the self-interpreted environment.

In addressing resiliency, we want to set up the theoretical framework to assist the individual. Protective factors can be identified to assist the client in developing positive responses to negative occurrences.

What are protective factors? Protective factors are also referred to as resilient factors or processes developed to help people succeed in spite of risk or challenge. These protective factors are generally viewed as external supports. The emphasis on ecological systems and ongoing relationships are used to bolster positive gains. Brooks and Goldstein[11] explain the importance of strategies to achieve a resilient mindset and stress hardiness using ten key concepts, which include:

1. Changing the words of life; rewriting your negative scripts
2. Choosing the path to become stress hardy rather than stressed out
3. Viewing life through the eyes of others
4. Communicating effectively
5. Accepting oneself and others
6. Making connections and displaying compassion
7. Dealing effectively with mistakes
8. Dealing well with success in building islands of competence
9. Developing self-discipline and self-control
10. Maintaining a resilient lifestyle

Taking the time to reflect upon external and internal changes experienced and redirecting your thoughts to focus on what was learned from those change have been shown to protect the individual. Thus, when I experience a negative event, if I reflect and deal with challenge Item 9—developing self-discipline and self-control—I will likely better care for myself and move forward with no long-term damage to myself. Referencing this list as it compares to the CMA constructs, we find that points Item 3—viewing life through other's eyes, Item 4—effective communication, Item 5—openness to accept self and others, and Item 7—effective management of mistakes have social cognitive (person, environment, and behavior) emphases. We are allowing an examination of the client's social environment to define challenges and we are examining strategies in response to the identified concerns. Item 2—selecting a strength-based plan to develop personalized hardiness and Item 10—maintaining a resilient lifestyle have a goal-oriented focus. This allows the client to define what that lifestyle will require to manage and maintain sustained success. Items 1—reframing to positive words that support and build-up a positive life, Item 6—have positive friends and associates so that you are able to receive and extend compassion, 8 – reflect and internalize success to build efficacy in achieving competence, and Item 9 – develop strategies and self-discipline that foster success; each of these are self-regulatory. It is not specific items that make up resiliency rather, it is the personalized substance of resiliency strategies and how challenges are managed that is of importance. The customized design to meet your clients' needs is the opportunity for you to help address the unique needs they may encounter from that point forward. The ecological, social cognitive, goal-oriented, self-regulation and engagement-style information you have collected will be used to customize your client's ideal protective factors in the form of mantras, which will facilitate future success. Your clients' growth and development plans are also included with the resiliency plan.

How do you incorporate the client's CMP data to develop a customized resiliency plan through self-regulation? Let's revisit Leah one last time to step through what might be her resiliency plan. Because each of the LIBRE Model problem-solving exchanges has provided detailed self-managed and regulated data, we will use that information as a basis for this presentation.

We have four problem-solving stick figures to identify ecological context and social systems that Leah has presented over the course of time together; the summary tables and the CMA documentation to summarize observations. Our planning begins as follows:

> Step 1: Self-regulation—Help Leah create a word collage of all of her encouraging phrases and others that she might want to reference in the future and encourage self-reflection, self-awareness, and self-management. Ownership is established by her design; urge her to place this representation on her room wall or select a choice location. Ecological systems and ongoing social relationships—identify with her self-reflective occasions throughout the day when she would be able to use her self-affirming phrases. Identify positive actions that she can take in association with the challenging situations. Identify what those challenging settings may include and then role-play how to use her phrase. For example, if she feels uncomfortable with the boyfriend's mother and her boyfriend, she may select to go study in the room (identify this as her cue to act), take a moment to review her collage, and read each of the phases aloud to herself. It will be OK. Then ask her to identify something specific to that reference point—it will be OK that I am feeling uncomfortable and move away, this gives me time to complete my studies so I will be able to graduate.
>
> Step 2: Engagement style—because Leah has demonstrated a preference to actual engagement, encourage her to journal about her feelings and thoughts. As she tracks what she feels, she is allowing herself to remain actually engaged. She will be able to continue to process, develop goals, and reflect on who she is and what she is becoming. If she records an unsuccessful event, encourage her to journal what she has learned from the experience. What from this experience that will facilitate future success? This too is a self-regulation and resilience strategy contextualized within her ecological system. You

are not judging her ecological systems; you are teaching her to evaluate her systems. She is learning and adjusting to maintain a future positive outlook.

Step 3: Social cognition and ecological (individual-within-community) interface—Leah has presented her environmental values and foci. We recorded her network of friends and family. We have four snapshot pictures of Leah: in her school environment, in her described home environment, she as a person, and Leah as she explores other potential behaviors. These interactions help with the development of several general social cognitive resilience statements, for example viewing life through the eyes of others provide support and developing self-discipline and self-control to provide her time and space to process her thoughts and feelings. Important here are the personalized proclamations that will assist Leah in creating statements that will reflect her specific context. For example, I am fortunate to have so many people caring about me: my teachers, my boyfriend, and my parents. I have a lot of options when I need to talk with someone. I am not alone. Her value is community and her ecological systems are set up with that orientation; we have affirmed that value and worked with her to create a new resiliency mantra that may be an action plan when she experiences future challenge or adversity. I am a good and strong person and I know how to take time to think before making a decision.

Step 4: Goal orientation—Leah has provided specific goals with associated values, so her protective factors should include her value to supporting those she loves rather than focusing on any judgment about her boyfriend. At your last meeting, she indicated a goal of creating balance. This goal can be used as the foundation for a number of strategies. You might ask her to begin by defining balance in terms of rest, school and social interactions. Give her homework of describing what balance might look like over the course of a week and then in a session together, write up daily balance tenets. For example, Leah may say, balance begins with a daily commitment to myself. Thus, this gives voice to her words, thoughts, and goals.

Step 5: Problem-solving—teaching Leah the steps to problem-solving has provided her the opportunity to slow down whatever she is experiencing so she will be able to incorporate her best thinking to make the best decision. It will be important to teach Leah to practice using this strategy whenever she encounters a challenge. She will likely continue to encounter challenges beyond those usually expected for her chronological age. Those possible challenges and how to approach them should be discussed. She may not have the answer, but you want to make sure she sees that she always has resources. You want to encourage Leah to invest in herself and to have confidence in her ability to make positive decisions to create a change in her life.

Table 10.1 Leah's Change over Time Presentation

Engagement Styles				
Session 1	*Session 2*	*Session 3*	*Session 4*	*Session 5*
Actual-engaged	Goal-focused engaged	Venting	Actual-engaged	Actual-engaged

Problem Orientation				
Session 1	*Session 2*	*Session 3*	*Session 4*	*Session 5*
Living situation	Family	Relationship with boyfriend	Relationship with boyfriend	Relationship with boyfriend
Boyfriend	School	Living situation	Living situation	School & my absences
School	Boyfriend		School	My family
Baby	Teachers		Baby	His family
				Living situation

Identified Themes and Goals		
	Theme Category	*Identified Goal*
Session 1	Personal	What can I do to support my boyfriend?
	Personal	Ask my boyfriend to meet at the grocery store so we can talk
		Decide what we are going to tell his mother and her boyfriend
		Decide what we are going to do if they don't pay
Session 2	Personal	When is the best time to talk with my boyfriend?
	Personal	Figure out my boyfriend's work schedule
		Make his lunch and ask him to call me at his lunch
		Meet him during his lunch
Session 3	Personal	What am I going to do about my living situation?
	Personal	I'm going to nap in the afternoon so I can be ready to visit with him when he gets home from work
		Ask him how he is doing and what I can do to help
		Do all of this tonight
Session 4	Personal	What do I need to do to prepare for the baby?

A wise elder professor once said, Aim for that golden gown as your goal and reach for it. You may not actually get the whole gown but even if you only get one golden thread, you will now have that golden thread and that is more than if you would have never pursued your goal.

Practice Client Exercise

Using the data that has been tracked, what would Leah's Resiliency Protective Factors include? What would Leah's resiliency plan address?

NOTES

1. Ellen A. Skinner and Jennifer Pitzer, "Developmental Dynamic of Engagement, Coping, and Everyday Resilience," in *Handbook of Research on Student Engagement,* edited by Sandra L. Christenson, Amy L. Reschly and Cathy Wyle (New York: Springer Science, 2012), 21–45.

2. James J. Appleton, Sandra L. Christenson and Michael J. Furlong, "Student Engagement with School: Critical Conceptual and Methodological Issues of the Construct," *Psychology in the Schools* 45, no. 5 (2008): 369–386.

3. Jennifer A. Fredricks, Phyllis C. Blumenfeld and Alison H. Paris, "School Engagement: Potential of the Concept, State of the Evidence," *Review of Educational Research* 74, no. 1(2004): 59–109.

4. Suniya S. Luthar, Dante Cicchetti and Brownyn Becker, "The Construct of Resilience: A Critical Evaluation and Guidelines for Future Work," *Child Development* 71, no. 3 (2000): 543.

5. Norman Gamezy, "Resiliency and Vulnerability to Adverse Developmental Outcomes Associated with Poverty," *American Behavioral Sciences* 34 (1991): 416–430.

6. Annemie Dillen, "The Resiliency of Children and Spirituality: A Practical Theological Reflection," *International Journal of Children's Spirituality* 17, no. 1 (2012): 61–75.

7. Ellen A. Skinner and Jennifer Pitzer, "Developmental Dynamic of Engagement, Coping, and Everyday Resilience," in *Handbook of Research on Student Engagement*, edited by Sandra L. Christenson, Amy L. Reschly and Cathy Wyle (New York: Springer Science, 2012), 21–45.

8. Urie Bronfenbrenner and Pamela A. Morris, "The Bioecological Model of Human Development," in *Theoretical Models of Human Development, Vol. 1 of the Handbook of Child Psychology* 5th ed., edited by Richard M. Lerner and William Damon (New York: Wiley, 2006), 793–828.

9. Sandra L. Christenson, Amy L Reschly and Cathy Wylie, eds., *Handbook of Research on Student Engagement* (New York: Springer, 2012).

10. Annemie Dillen, "The Resiliency of Children and Spirituality: A Practical Theological Reflection," *International Journal of Children's Spirituality* 17, no. 1 (2012): 61–75.

11. Robert Brooks and Sam Goldstein, *The Power of Resilience: Achieving Balance, Confidence, and Personal Strength in Your Life* (New York: McGraw-Hill, 2003), 10.

Chapter 11

Case Management Portfolio

It is quite eye opening for the clients to see their own words as concrete examples of self.

Objective: To examine the purpose and function of the Case Management Portfolio (CMP) in assisting the clinician and the client.

The Case Management Portfolio (CMP) is the case folder that contains all the client collected data, LIBRE Model problem-solving activity worksheets, completed Case Management Approach (CMA) session forms and any constructed tables or charts used to monitor client changes. This chapter addresses the CMP: how to use the CMP information to monitor and manage your client's case, make referrals, and closeout the case. This chapter discusses when to construct data-trend tables to assist with client management and what the clinician's role is in data management. The chapter closes with an examination of the clinician's role in data management and accountability.

The CMP is the ongoing repository of client data. The CMP's significance is grounded in the systematic manner in which data are collected and records are maintained. At each session, client data is collected and the CMA form completed to facilitate the documentation progress. Once completed, these forms are added to the CMP. Goals are set. Over time, these materials become resources for ongoing use. The client's responses to the LMSFT hold key information, not only for the clinician but also for the client. Clients' words can be used as a powerful intervention tool. For example, using the client's expressed problem-solving word patterns can facilitate client self-awareness. It is quite eye opening for the clients to see their own words as concrete examples of self. As one client reacted, Wow, I can't believe how many times I said I don't know what to do. The clients' own words become that initial engagement from which self-management strategies can be introduced. Over time, the clients' words cause an even more profound awakening when the client sees changes made to thinking as presented through problem-solving. The data allows the clients to see their own words and thoughts as positive change or evidence of any unwillingness to move beyond their current position. Clients have reported that it is affirming and motivational to see change in their own words.

For the clinician, having this source is important in identifying and monitoring client goals and change or other clinical decision making. For instance, the recorded data facilitates decisions about client progress or provides concrete examples of limited progress that may lead to outside referral for additional services. Data should be the basis for all mental health services and having the clients' words as data samples facilitates service. Further, if the client is a minor and a parent or guardian is requesting information, having the minor's words or expressions can aid in the communication with the parent or guardian. The same advantage is found when you're called into the legal system to speak to your client's well-being. Your records must be evidence-based; using the client's words fulfills that requirement. Because the majority of your records are primarily the client's exact words and responses to questions posed, you are tracking first level data.

Depending on the amount of time spent with a client, longitudinal data (even after two sessions) is collected and tracked. Self-identified goals assist with deciding on what content should be monitored. Constructing a table of the client's identified concerns addressed through each problem-solving activity and proposed resolutions can provide valuable data. You may also want to track social cognitive statements associated with their self-identified challenges. Engagement style information is an additional element that should be tracked. Finally, it is important to maintain a running summary that addresses client formative and summative evaluations.

The CMP begins with a table of contents that will assist with the management of key documents. The referral, the CMA session forms, which are completed with each session, and developed tables are the primary documents. There are CMA elements that may be extracted from the primary documents and placed in separate tables; for instance, how you calibrated your engagement style to best keep your client's motivated investment. Summary data is used to monitor progress and to close the case. As you develop the client management portfolio, a skeletal outline will assist and may include the following:

I. CMP Table of Content—Listing of all case management sections.
II. Referral—Introductory materials provided to the service provider prior to receiving a client. Includes the client's name, age, background, and other pertinent information.
III. CMA Form—Documentation of the organizing structure and managing track of the client's identified social context, goals, and engagement style orientation, maintained within the client-clinician communication.

IV. Tables of Change over Time—Tabular representations of client or other pertinent information that is being tracked over time.
V. Resilience Plan—Individualized plan to assist client with sustaining positive changes.
VI. Summary—Formative evaluations that monitor smaller changes, ongoing assessed changes, and summative evaluations—monitor larger goal changes, particularly at the closing of client progress.

CMP Use

To illustrate how the CMP can assist in organizing, planning, and providing services, let's assume you work with an ongoing case involving a novice teacher. Jake, a recent university graduate was hired to teach history in a low-income school district. He was pleased that he was able to find a job so quickly; however, the significant challenges he is experiencing have left him feeling insecure. He decided that unless he sought some external help, he might find himself alone and without a job.

Referral

You have been working with Jake for a year and eight months. He ultimately referred himself for services because he felt like everything in his life was out of control. He is thirty-six years old. He is a middle-school teacher. He reports that his students are not learning. Jake indicates that he has no real problems at home, but he feels out of control and has no idea what more he can do. His wife suggested he consider counseling because she is tired of hearing him complain about everything that he is experiencing.

Clinician Calibrated Engagement

Initially when you began to see Jake, you entered the session from an actual engagement style; however, you quickly learned that Jake has a strong goal-focused engagement style preference. When you first noticed the preference, you decide to begin tracking the dominance. You have labeled this table Engagement Styles over Time, and you adjusted your entry with each session to that of a goal-focused engagement style.

LIBRE Model Problem-Solving Stick Figure Worksheets

Jake comes in once a month to discuss what is occurring in his life. He reports that he likes problem-solving, so he has asked for the opportunity to complete the LIBRE Model with each of his sessions. Jake's goal is to improve his personal management. To assist in the data management a table was created. The Problem Orientation addresses what he defines as his primary problem—what we spend time processing as his main concern. The Identified Themes tracks whether the problem was personal involving his wife, daughter, or home concerns; school-related involving his students; or work-related challenges with his co-teachers, professional development, and administration. The Identified Themes is used to track the social cognitive statements that he used to encourage himself. While you may select to track any number of data points, engagement styles, identified problems and problem themes are easily extracted from the LIBRE Model SFTs.

Table of Client Information

Identified goals may assist with deciding what data to track. For Jake, a change of time table was developed and information tracked. You have made the commitment to share the table with Jake every six months so he might identify patterns among challenges and social cognitive statements as well as the engagement style used to approach each.

Intervention

Systematic problem-solving and monitoring of his challenges has occurred. As a self-referred client, he indicated that he just wanted to have someone to talk to about what he has been experiencing and how he has managed each situation. Working with his engagement style, you were able to help him better appreciate his personal strengths. For example, most goal-focused clients plan to be productive. Your understanding of his engagement style will facilitate and provide him self-monitoring information about his learning and skill development. As you provide him this insight, he will likely be pleased because even if he never acknowledged his engagement style, hearing it spoken to him, it does ring true. Jake's progress was affirming and motivating for him. Over an extended period of time, the table is evidence of client gains. The results of these sessions have been collected. The created table (Table 11.1) content has his reported concerns. These compiled data points were shared with Jake. You discuss his self-managed gains and together develop a resiliency plan.

Clinician's Role in Data Management and Accountability

The advantage of the LIBRE Model problem-solving activity and the CMP is that they provide a variety of data elements that can be tracked from social cognitive information to how clients identify problems—within their control or outside their control—and their willingness to set goals and develop resolution plans. The included formative data was collected as the client's progress was measured. The CMP is your organizing repository. The evaluation included both observations and changes as reported by Jake. Summative data was collected once Jake's overall goal was achieved. Your willingness to track the client's data can enable you to make more informed goals, interventions, and treatment plans. Your willingness to remain accountable to your clients will facilitate the entire process.

Summary

The CMP is best explained within the context of this collected data use. The portfolio assists the clinician in tracking client gains and set backs. It also is a visual tool that can be used to help the client identify patterns in content themes, challenges and how they are managed. In this case, Jake is able to see his own strengths and vulnerabilities. He views his words and plans. Together you are able to review those plans (completed and/or not completed). He is able to see evidence of change and that facilitates his identified goal to better self-manage. These successes have allowed him the feedback (using his own words) to develop the self-regulation and management skills. His resiliency plan is constructed from this foundation. At the same time, the CMP data is available for clinician use in reference to any report writing and/or inquiry.

As you review Jake's record of work, you note positive personal, school, and work changes that address the identified goal. His decisions have been tracked. He reports that he now believes he has better control over his life. With each session, a review of his resolution plans has been conducted. He has reported that he followed through and has provided detail to the results; this suggests that he has held himself accountable. You used his own positive expressions of affirmation in speaking with him. Jake is continuing to make gains, and he reports that he feels like he finally has things under his control. You introduced the importance of self-management and building a strong support in developing his social cognitive resilience, and you will focus on several techniques. This data suggests that the client should be able to self-manage with little to no support. Jake has learned how to problem solve and self-regulate. You anticipate releasing him as a client soon.

When should a table be constructed? Construct a table when you will have to make and/or defend (support) clinical decisions. You may find a predominant concern that continues to surface; tables allow you to track the frequency and any other deemed appropriate detail. You may then address this as tabularized information (sub-goal or as it occurs in relation to the client's goal). Once you determine the client's range for improvement (Vygotsky's Zone of Proximal Development), the table can be used to reflect those goal(s) and sub-goals. To assist you with deciding what to track, you may select to begin with: identified concerns, identified goals, developed resolution plans and engagement styles. In Jake's case, he was goal-focused in most of the sessions. His expectation was that he would be given an opportunity to problem solve, revisit prior plans and be able to engage in new skills and strategies for better personal management.

Practice Client Exercise

Using the practice client you created in administering the LIBRE Model, use that data collected to set-up a table to reflect key information that you would deem important to be included in a CMP.

Table 11.1 Change over Time Presentation

Year 1	Year 2
Engagement Styles over Time	
Jake	
Potential	Goal-focused
Potential	Goal-focused
Potential	Goal-focused
Goal-focused	Goal-focused
Goal-focused	Goal-focused
Goal-focused	Potential
Goal-focused	Goal-focused
Goal-focused	Goal-focused
Goal-focused	
Goal-focused	
Goal-focused	
Goal-focused	
Problem Orientation	
Self-school	Working with other students
School	Working with other students
School	Home
School	Self
Self	Working with other students
Self	Self
Self	Students
Self	
Self	
Self	
Self	
Identified Themes	
Theme Category	*Social-Cognitive Statements*
Personal	Keep up
Personal	Let my friends take the lead
Personal	Continue with support
Personal	Breakdown house by rooms; pick day to begin picking up
Personal	Go on a couple of *dates* with wife
Personal	Get daughter ready and take her to sitter
School-related	Don't trash anything
School-related	Make spreadsheet of activities
School-related	Spend two hours on Saturday looking for resources
School-related	Use good resource from last year
Work-related	Sign up for practice exam
Work-related	Contact state
Work-related	Try to avoid their *talking* as best I can
School-related	Remember that students were like this before me
School-related	Start looking for resources this weekend
Work-related	Talk with counselor
Work-related	Speak to lead teacher
Work-related	Will e-mail lead teacher
Work-related	Will apply for additional professional development
Work-related	Keep conversations with other teachers to business only

Chapter 12

Working Under Supervision

Your professional development is an imperative investment in yourself as a service provider and clinician.

Objective: To address the use of LIBRE problem-solving Model and engagement within supervision.

This chapter addresses the clinician–supervisor relationship using the LIBRE Model problem-solving exchange to monitor content and professional development goals. Salient LIBRE Model responses provide the supervisor a records-based view of the supervisee's client case management. Similar to client tracking implemented by the clinician, the supervisor assists the supervisee in defining the PDP. This PDP will include the philosophical and theoretical service orientations, supervisee professional gains, resolution challenges and new skills acquired. The PDP is the supervisee's portfolio used to organize delineated goals and to record contracted clinician–supervisor service parameters. We discuss the shared accountability of the supervisee and supervisor, each maintaining distinct roles in support of the supervisee's professional success. Also addressed is the PDP portfolio and its function as a case-evidenced-based example of skill and professional development.

Supervisee Goals

The first step toward establishing a focused supervisee–supervisor relationship involves the identification of a supervisor. Consider the type of skills and experiences that you would want your supervisor to have and consider the skills you want for yourself. Your supervisor functions much like a mentor and will be the person who facilitates your professional development. Take the time necessary to shop around to identify a person you feel comfortable with;

identify a professional persona. Look for professionals you are able to ask questions freely of without feeling compromised or embarrassed. This is one of the most important professional contracts you will make. Select someone you want to learn from and practice with; consider this a one-on-one training. Your professional development is an imperative investment in yourself as a service provider and clinician. This essential investment is not only for yourself professionally, but also for the impact you will have on future clients. Be clear with your goals. Be able to identify your professional purpose, philosophy and ideals. Spend time to conduct value assessments. This will work as the foundation and underpinning to who you are and to who you want to become. You may set this as your first agenda item with your supervisor once you identify that person. Don't be afraid to move into a learning or student role as you work with your supervisor. Most professional groups work under some type of apprenticeship. Seize this opportunity to create this professional commitment. Above all remember that mentees do one day become mentors, too.

Supervisee–Supervisor Relationship

This is a shared relationship between the supervisee and supervisor; each carries specific responsibility in managing the professional relationship. The supervisee comes to each meeting prepared to discuss clinical notes and clients' identified challenges. While the clinician usually maintains a monitoring role, in the supervisee–supervisor session, it is the supervisor who monitors the session. This frees the supervisee to express and process personal or professional challenges.

There are a variety of relational processing challenges that may arise within the supervisor–supervisee exchange. Three examples are provided to illustrate this subtle interaction. The first involves a supervisee–clinician who works with trauma victims and has recently found himself experiencing similar symptoms to his clients. The literature has a number of terms to reference this behavior, from compassion fatigue, secondary traumatic stress (STS) to secondary traumatic stress disorder (STSD), which occurs among those service providers who work closely with individuals who have experienced trauma.[1] Returning to this example, the established client-clinician relationship is the place for this at-risk clinician to be given time to process the exposure and impact of time spent with that traumatized client.[2] If the supervisee is unaware of the personal risk, the supervisor may be the person who identifies the concern in communication with the supervisee.

A second example involves unresolved issues that may surface while in the service provider role. You as the supervisee may find that a client leaves you feeling that you need help too; perhaps a client reminds you of a loved one you have lost. While it is never appropriate to process your need (grief) with a client, it is appropriate to spend time with your supervisor working through those unresolved emotions, feelings or thoughts.

A third example of how best to use the supervisor–supervisee relationship involves learning new skills and interventions. For example, you have a client in session that continues to exhibit troublesome behavior and all of the appropriate techniques to engage her in deeper conversation are not enough. While you determined from the client responses that the client was sad rather than depressed, you were still bothered by where the client was and are now asking questions of yourself and your supervisor. What should I have done? Is there something that I should have introduced to this client that could have assisted her in thinking or processing that change? This special time allows the supervisor to collaborate with you, as an external consultant, to self-reflect and examine the session, your self-awareness, and the expressed remaining concern.

The PDP (PDP as outlined in chapter 4) provides a great advantage for you and the management of your supervision. You may ask why you would want to bring this plan into the supervisory relationship. Your PDP can be used as a supervisee–supervisor contract supplement. Sessions can be tracked and data collected (onto the PDP) that can then be used to trace through session gains and setbacks. This will assist with the defining of the relationship. Similar to sessions with your clients, but at a trainer-of-trainers level. The PDP becomes that accountability document. In addition, the supervisor can help you as the supervisee–clinician to process troublesome client-contextualized data and services. Together, other options can be explored and additional perceptions considered. As opportunity arises, new skills may be taught and practiced with your supervisor. This safe, protected relationship holds the same level of confidentiality as a counseling session and thus, can be used to process occurrences that cannot be processed elsewhere.

Supervisee–Supervisor Parameters

Addressing as many parameters as is possible when establishing the supervisee–supervisor relationship will facilitate your contracted time with your supervisor or supervisee. It is wise to discuss what and how the time will be used up front. For instance, you as a supervisee have agreed that you will share all information with your supervisor with the understanding that she will listen and process before moving quickly to correct your approach—or you may prefer the opposite. You explain that you want to be told the rationale associated with a professional correction and you provide an example, saying, please don't tell me—I never want to be told, don't ever cry when the client begins to cry. You explain to your supervisor that being told not to cry is not enough, you want to be told why a given behavior is inappropriate or how it will introduce risk. This then sets up an operational parameter for your relationship.

Of course, you must know yourself as a student or supervisee prior to requesting these types of parameters, so invest time in self-reflection. Consider the ideal learning setting and ask your supervisor for those setting conditions. Be aware that your supervisor may also come requesting specific parameters. An example for the supervisor may be as follows: You agree to work with your supervisee as skills are being developed; however, each time you visit with the supervisee to discuss client and personal progress, the supervisee reverts to a potential engagement and checks out, offering excuses for not making any changes.

As the supervisor, you may select to have a parameter that specifies that you will work with your supervisee as long as he or she is invested in the working relationship, however, if you see that the time together is not profiting, you may let your supervisee know that you are prepared to terminate the supervision. While not every parameter can be addressed in advance, having basic ground rules will facilitate the communication and learning process.

Supervisor–Supervise Agreed upon Ground Rules

Together, you may decide to have a general agenda that will be introduced with each session. One example is as follows:

1. Check-in to address where, how, and what the supervisee has experienced since the last meeting; this can be accomplished using the LIBRE Model problem-solving activity. This will also assist you in monitoring your engagement style in working with your supervisor.
2. Address one specific case that has been challenging.
3. Discuss alternative intervention directions that may assist.
4. Learn and practice a new skill and evaluate gains made.
5. Set a plan for new approaches that will be implemented. This may include homework for the supervisee.

The more defined the time-in-session, the more profitable it will be for all involved. Once the parameters and meeting framework are established, those agreed-upon tenets can be added to the supervisee PDP and become a reference point for both parties. This will allow the relationship to grow with the established goals and within the predetermined parameters. You may also want to make the agreement more official by having both parties sign and date the recorded document. Finally, if you are contracting for a specific time, let's say one year, goals are set for three, six, nine, and twelve months so you will be able to work from novice to intermediate to advanced supervisee to an expert supervisee. These become evaluative measures that can be monitored for progress gains.

Supervisor as a Facilitator

The supervisor is an external catalyst for change, maintaining accountability, fostering new skills and introducing ethical questions, considerations and scenarios for discussion. It is the supervisor's role to create and maintain a table of topics and skills that will be addressed. Your supervisor is able to assist you in meeting your identified needs even as you have and continue to assist your clients. The supervisor will help you develop more expert skills. The supervisor is not a friend; dual relationships will only jeopardize the learning experience. For example, you ask your licensed friend if she will supervise you and because she is your friend, she feels obligated to agree. However, before long, your supervisee-friend sees that you are engaging in several unethical practices and when she attempts to bring it to your attention, you are offended. I thought you were my friend, you say under your breath. A better scenario is the supervisor and supervisee who have no other acquaintance other than that of the single professional development relationship.

Supervisee as an Expert-in-Training

Remembering that one day soon, you will be the expert in practice helps to keep a perspective and it should fortify your supervisor selection. Your goal should include skills used by experts in the field that you have not had an opportunity to learn through formal coursework. You may want to add skills and experiences into the supervisory contract that address those specific counseling orientations. Ask yourself, who are the individuals conducting evidence-based research in the field and what skills are they implementing? Then work with your supervisor to ensure that there is facilitated assistance for you to gain those skills.

Professional Development Plan

Keeping track of self-regulated engagement styles is important. Awareness of engagement both with clients and when working with the supervisor offers key insights to what and how you self-manage while providing services and how best to care for self. Supervisee Brenda has worked with her supervisor Fran to monitor Brenda's engagement with each of her clients and together they complete the LIBRE Model activity to identify her engagement styles within the supervisee session. This information has allowed Brenda to be self-reflective and she reports that she is comfortable with being able to cognitively shift to meet her clients' needs. Fran tracks Brenda's engagement styles (recording the information on Brenda's PDP) to better assist her with her own mental wellness and care of self. Philosophically, Brenda wants to approach her supervision from an inquiry-based humanistic approach, as she sees herself as a discovery learning professional and self-starter. Brenda and Fran agree upon this approach and Fran informs Brenda that the problem-solving LIBRE Model will allow her that self-management.

Together they establish a general agenda outline (to compliment the ground rules) for their supervisory meetings:

1. Check-in (LIBRE Model activity)—Fran administers the LIBRE Model to Brenda as an initial activity with each meeting.
2. Case review—a case of Fran's selection will be reviewed and discussed. Fran comes prepared to introduce a topic associated with the case. Together they discuss the client's responses to the LIBRE Model. They address Brenda's notes and reference the client's CMP.
3. Work with one of her three identified goals: (1) targeted learning will involve becoming culturally competent, (2) learning how to provide services using the Response to Intervention (RTI) Framework, and (3) learning the necessary skills to become a bilingual licensed school psychologist. Depending on the time spent in reviewing the case, Fran will introduce either a new skill or discussion in reference to one of the three goals. Fran always comes prepared to address one of the goals during their session.
4. Closing will always include a review of Brenda's PDP and evaluate Brenda's gains in terms of skills used with clients and the agreed upon plan of focus for their next meeting. If they agree on homework (for example, practicing a new intervention with a client) it will be added to their agenda for their next meeting. An example of this meeting may begin with the review of her PDP, focusing first on her strengths—assessment, being bilingual, and her role as a school psychologist counselor. As they review her anticipated challenges—balancing school, work, and continuing her education coursework—Fran begins to work with Brenda to explore what she can do to balance her many commitments. Together they review her time commitments. Brenda pulls out her calendar and begins making notes. They discuss time management and Brenda creates a plan for next week.

As the dialogue continues, Brenda addresses not only her challenges but also her anticipated risk—not satisfying the RTI Framework goal through practicum. Together Fran and Brenda begin to develop a plan that will ensure that she has the RTI experience without solely depending on her practicum. Brenda appears more relaxed after they outline her plan to acquire RTI experience.

Fran compliments Brenda on her in-service training and asks her if this is a population she wants to work with at some point in the future. Brenda says yes, she believes this training has helped her become more culturally competent in working with this population. They review Brenda's pending coursework, personal defined workshop goals and/or ongoing CEU (continuing educational units) commitments. They close their session with Brenda's specific time management plan to balance her professional and personal investments. They agree on the time and date of their next meeting and close the session.

Fran updates Brenda's engagement table and identified challenges with the anticipation that Fran will continue to improve on her self-regulated use of time and professional development. This PDP allows Brenda to see her progress over time and should also provide her encouragement as she invests in her profession and herself. For Fran, the PDP provides documentation of the time investment made in Brenda's professional development and the skills, interventions, and professional topics addressed over their contracted time. By the time the relationship closes, each will have gained from the relationship and the investment in tracking those changes.

As we close this chapter and review key points, understand that you will begin as a novice and progress to an intermediate and then an advanced-level clinician; so it will be important to grow and develop the relationship by investing in the partnership. This is accomplished by shifting from student-supervisee to colleague-supervisee; work together with your supervisor so that neither feels threatened by the change over time. Coming with new techniques or skills that are then shared with the supervisor is one natural way to approach this change. The structure placed on the supervisory relationship will facilitate the learning and accountability. Create a supervisory relationship that will work for you.

Summary

1. Establish criteria in selecting a supervisor. Develop a personal professional philosophical statement that addresses your professional beliefs, values, and purpose.
2. The supervisory relationship needs parameters to function efficiently.
3. The supervisee should be prepared to share any and all cases with the supervisor.
4. The supervisor commits to track key supervisee information and supervisee progress as components of the PDP. For example, the supervisor may track the supervisee's LIBRE Model engagement styles and identified challenges.

5. From the problem-solving CMA, the supervisor will encourage self-development through reflection.
6. The supervisor will offer new techniques, interventions, and professional development observations.
7. The supervisor–supervisee is a shared partnership and with each session agendas will be developed for the following session.
8. A review of the PDP goals will occur with each session.
9. The supervisee should be comfortable to explore personal and professional challenges with the supervisor as they occur. The relationship content is confidential.
10. Evaluative measures should be set up to monitor the supervisee's progress. Incorporate homework as needed, and make sure that it is added to the agenda for the next meeting.

NOTES

1. Charles R. Figley, "Trauma Stress: The Role of the Family and Social Support System," in *Trauma and its Theory, Research, and Intervention*, edited by Charles R. Figley (New York: Brunner/Mazel, 1986): 39–54.
2. Charles R. Figley, ed., *Treating Stress in Families* (New York: Brunner/Mazel, 1989).

Chapter 13

Engagement Styles in Consultation[1]

The establishment of a teamed partnership is critical to any consultation approach.

Objective: To examine the use of problem-solving and engagement within consultation.

Consultation involves a collaborative exchange between consultants and direct service providers,[2] in which the core characteristic is the consultant-consultee partnership. This working unit comes together to process identified problems and develop solutions. While new consultation models continue to be added to the field, consultant-consultee communication remains a pivotal skill set that can be used in response to immediate (consultative) need. Here we'll look at this model in the context of the education system. The principles will be applicable to other consultative relationships.

There exists over thirty years of history of school-teaming collaborative efforts[3] with the commitment to refine student or system impact. For instance, in the ecological-behavioral problem-solving model, which involves the use of relevant existing school and family systems information in combination with behavioral elements to address students' identified concerns, Gutkin[4] explains this eco-behavioral shift (away from traditional behavioral systems) as an active approach to integrating the student's whole-person context. Bandura[5] asserts that within the patterns of person, environment, and behavioral reciprocal interaction, social cognitive learning becomes predictable. The ecological-behavioral consultative application affords opportunity to explore identified problems within a larger context, possibly including increased self-awareness, self-regulation, and cognitive expression by the participants. The exhibited behaviors of the student, as well as the teacher, are examined within the social school system.

The teacher and the student become equal contributors to the challenge and solution. At a larger scale, in spite of possible benefits, potential risks are introduced to the teachers. The open-ended nature of this indirect ecological-behavioral service model may introduce personal fear of potential consequence.[6] What will occur when the larger picture is examined, and the teacher is identified as the one needing to change? This resulting sense of vulnerability compounds the problem.

The establishment of a teamed partnership is critical to any consultation approach. The LIBRE Model problem-solving approach can be used to facilitate consultant-consultee communication. The strength-based nature of the model provides the consultee (teacher) a controlled dialogue in which to identify the worldviews of the problem, of self, of values, and of the student. The consultee is free to vent, provide social context, and identify goals in relationship to other competing challenges that may either support safeguards or introduce additional vulnerability.

Whether consultation involves mainstream students[7] or RTI services, educator participation is important.[8] Sustainability of effective services will link back to teachers and the roles they maintain in the implementation of services. In spite of the skilled participation of counselors, educational diagnosticians and school psychologists, it is the teachers who hold a critical role in implementation and they cannot be minimized, marginalized, or victimized in the process.

LIBRE Model as a Responsive Consultative Tool

The LIBRE model is designed to provide a self-managed intervention to a specified challenge. The teacher maintains personal security and control over the activity. The consultant offers the scripted LIBRE Model prompts to the teacher. Processed one-step at a time, the problem-solving activity provides a sounding board to process and develop goals and action plans. The completed LIBRE Model record provides the consultant information in regard to the consultee's views of the problem and willingness to develop a goal, plan, and ultimate resolution. Clinical observation of client's responses to the scripted cues has been found to facilitate greater understanding of the ecological complexity related to the problem, as well as provide an understanding of the degree of teacher investment, personal attention, goal-setting, likelihood of persistence, and willingness to change.[9]

The LMSFT functions as a protocol guide and record form.[10] The LMSFT includes respondent prompts to focus the individual on the problem and away from self as a component of the challenge. Hidi and Berndorff[11] and Hidi and Harackiewicz[12] explain that situational interest operates as an external trigger to the integration of internalization through conscious decisions. Similarly, the LIBRE Model becomes a conduit to the person's personal eco-behavioral system and an expression of that system. Bandura suggests value to active participation with his statement, "consciousness is the very substance of mental life that not only makes life personally manageable but worth living."[13]

In the first step of the LIBRE Model, Listen, the teacher is asked to examine and identify pressing issues. The second step, Identify, provides the teacher the opportunity to choose the most pressing issue for which he or she is seeking assistance. Brainstorming allows the teacher the freedom to explore potential options to the presented problem. Because this stage casts the framework for brainstorming, the teacher is encouraged to provide options regardless of viability. The intention is to encourage divergent, creative thought. The teacher is supported and encouraged to generate as many options as possible. Here some participants identify need for additional information or other resources. Reality-testing involves asking the teacher to consider implications of the solutions proposals generated. The final step, Encourage, prompts the teacher to develop a suitable action plan.

A multidimensional investment introduced by the LIBRE Model is illustrated by the dimensions of initial and sustained attention. These apportioned attentions offer the consultant insight in how best to work with the teacher. Take for example a teacher who expresses a focused communication on the observed problem behavior rather than consider any additional other expanded consideration. The language used to express the challenge operates as an indicator (e.g., active or passive, global or specific) of willingness to follow through with generated resolutions (or not). The consultant will find that by honing in on these subtle teacher messages, the relationship will assume different directions. Throughout the process, the consultant notes teacher responsiveness, investment, and level of participation, which at the close will be measured as one of the four engagement styles described in chapter 7.

Remember these engagement styles are made up of two levels of attention: initial attention and sustained attention. Knowing this helps the consultant adjust to the consultee. If the consultant aligns his or her personal communication and worldview with the consultee, the consultee is likely to respond with an increased level of rapport. The consultant can use the consultee's schema, instructional efficacy, and language to better define problem interventions. From this vantage, the consultant works more effectively with the consultee to achieve the collaborative rapport necessary for a successful consultation. Because the LIBRE Model is problem-focused, the client operates collegially rather than from a deficiency perspective, thereby creating a greater likelihood of consultee acceptance.

Engagement styles address initial and sustained attentiveness toward self-awareness and goal orientation. The LIBRE Model is used to identify this by highlighting underlying scripts that reflect mores, cultural values, and prior experience in problem-solving. The construct of sustained attention provides a further elaboration of the individuals' willingness to hold a self-managed problem-solving investment. In earlier clinical work, sustained attentiveness appeared as reflections of goal orientation.[14] The LIBRE Model problem-solving activity facilitates inquiry and the identification of individual preferences.

See the table under Engagement Style Investment in chapter 7, which shows how LIBRE Model responses indicate initial and sustained attention.

Engagement Style Consultations

Four teacher consultation profiles are provided as examples of consultee's responses in using the LMSFT to identify engagement styles, beginning with the most invested level of responsiveness with the actual engaged, to the least engaged potential.

Actual Engaged Teacher Consultative Response

The actual engaged teacher welcomed the use of the LIBRE Model with a sense of anticipation. The teacher was cognizant of a need for external assistance and was ready to begin the session. Presented responses to the Listen prompt suggested awareness and attentiveness, which set the stage for the consultant's introduction of the Identify prompt, which then led to a presentation of one issue which was formulated as a question for discussion: How do I meet the varied special needs in the classroom? This was followed by myriad responses to the Brainstorm prompt that then lead to Reality-testing. There was a moment's pause before the teacher began stating the details and concerns. Finally, the session concluded with a detailed resolution plan and timeline to the Encourage prompt. The session moved with minimum consultant prompting beyond the standard questions, and the pace was swift and lively.

Goal-focused Teacher Consultative Response

The goal-focused engaged teacher was stoic as the session began. With crossed arms, the teacher waited to see how the consultative interview would proceed. When prompted to respond to the LIBRE Model Listen prompt, the consultee was quick to identify the student of concern. No other items were offered, so they then moved to the second prompt of Identify a presenting issue, which resulted in the question, how do I get Johnny to stay seated? The teacher took a deep breath when asked to Brainstorm options. This time, however, she moved to uncross arms and began to list all the different possibilities. The teacher offered eight possible responses to the stated question.

She moved to Reality-testing with anticipation when asked, Now what would it look like if you did assume that option? As the reality-testing prompt was offered, responses flowed as a list of detailed considerations and with implications to each brainstormed option. By the time the teacher reached the Encourage prompt, she felt confident in the management of the process. The teacher was pleased and offered a word of thanks for the consultant's listening and willingness to value the problem-solving exchange.

Venting Teacher Consultative Response

The venting engaged teacher entered the session with a cordial smile and was ready to begin. The teacher's quick response came as a list of detailed events that resulted in the consultant visit. She offered great detail to the context, class setting, and the pressures that were being experienced as a result of the student. As they moved from the Listen to the Identify a presenting issue, her voice tone and body language changed. She indicated that it was difficult for her to identify just one concern: There are too many. I don't know where to begin. The teacher went back to listing additional concerns and again explained that she was having a great number of problems and that she was at a loss as to where to begin. She finally asked the consultant; can't you just tell me what and where to begin? The consultant encouraged her to select one and again offered the Identify prompt. There was not much better return with the second prompt. After some time, the teacher said, I don't know that I can do anything more than I have, and I just don't know what I'm going to do. The session closed here. The consultant restated the information that had been provided and explained that her goal was to address both her thoughts and possible actions. So she indicated that this would be where they would begin in the development of a resolution plan in response to the current context. No specific issue was identified and no resolution plan was developed.

Potential Teacher Consultative Response

The potential engaged teacher began the session from a compliant stance. She was neither invested nor overly willing to participate. Once she was offered the first prompt, her response was simple: I feel overwhelmed with everything taking place in the classroom. The consultant asked her to offer some examples or details of what she was experiencing. The teacher's reply was direct: There is too much going on in the class. So the consultant then offered the next prompt: Identify a presenting issue. The response was, how do I handle feeling overwhelmed and what do I do with everything that is going on in the classroom? From this broad question, they moved to the Brainstorm prompt, from which she offered little new information. As the consultant asked her to address the Reality-testing, she had nothing new to offer. As they moved to the Encourage prompt, the teacher indicated that she felt hopeless. I need to do something but I don't know where to begin.

Responsiveness to Identified Engagement Styles

The responses to consultative problem-solving provide cues to better ground the relationship and the development of rapport. For the actual engaged consultee, the consultant's role is likely to require relatively minimal instruction. The teacher with this engagement style is highly motivated and invested in addressing the problem from both the individual and broader context.

For the goal-focused engagement style consultee there is a minimum initial investment but significant self-reflection. Therefore, much like the consultant effort related to actual engaged consultee, the goal-focused individual is likely willing to extend sufficient motivation in developing strong action plans. With this type of client it is possible to expect relatively successful consultation outcomes with minimal consultant instruction.

In response to the venting engagement style, the consultant will be required to a make a larger investment in the consultation. The teacher is more willing to be emotive and process rather than to explore and invest in change. The consultant will need to monitor time and introduce goal-setting consideration as problematic concerns are discussed.

The final consultative example is that of the potential engagement style that requires the largest time investment. The consultant should expect to spend

Table 13.1 Engagement Style Consultative Investment Plan

Engagement Style	*Consultant Input*	*Consultant Tools*
Actual	Minimal time for maximum consultee return	Active listening, supportive encouragement
Goal-Focused	Encourage goal focus with summary that includes values to environment scan	Active listening, reflection, supports to goal-setting with instruction to attend to environmental cues
Venting	Place time limits on venting to begin teaching goal-setting and management	Active listening, summary, and re-statement, goal-setting and management instruction.
Potential	Maximum time for small return	Active listening, goal-setting instruction, reflection, role-play practice, supportive monitoring, error analysis

some time just getting to know the teacher—values, experience, and culture—before any further investment occurs. Although this engagement style consultee may appear uninterested, alternate possibilities should be considered and explored. If this person has had limited problem-solving experience, this may demonstrate limited investment in exploring alternate solutions to the problem. It may be the case that the individual is reflecting language and behaviors often associated with individuals who lack confidence or experience. The consultant should prepare to offer instructional time and modeled practice.

Incorporation of Consultee's Engagement Style for Increased Rapport

From the onset of the consultation, consultee engagement style information is valuable as a communication consideration as well as a means for directing the eco-behavioral intervention. Investing the time to understand the client's investment is important in establishing rapport. In using the LIBRE Model, attending to the Listen response offers cues to the individual's personal self-attention and social setting. The client who is able to state the problem during the Identify step suggests a greater investment and focus on the one item of concern. This may be an indication that the teacher only wants to visit on the subject. In contrast, if the teacher is unable to identify one problem, the level of investment may not be present. This behavioral presentation suggests someone who actually does not want to consider change options. Only once the stated question is provided may one's investment be assumed. The willingness to explore a specific problem becomes an indicator of goal investment. The Brainstorming provides insight to consultee willingness to explore creative, divergent thought. The greater the number of consultee-generated options, the greater the clients suggested continued investment. The Reality-testing step is designed to explore convergent thinking related to possible and plausible solutions. In analyzing the information provided, attendant consequences considered and stated become contemplated reflection of each option if acted upon. Finally with the Encourage step, the individual develops a plan. Here the critical factors related to style are the participant's approach and detail with which the plan is offered.

While the actual and goal-focused engaged teachers are prepared to act on the identified challenge, the venting and potential engaged teachers are not. The differences have direct implications as to how the consultant will proceed with their subsequent sessions. For the venting and potential engaged teachers the session will move more slowly; for the actual and goal-focused the process will move with a more direct goal-oriented stance.

Discussion

These patterned results have been found in earlier research.[15] When given the opportunity to express their thoughts and discuss their student's behaviors in their own words and as defined within their own social context, teachers say as much about themselves as they do about the students they're working with. The opportunity to examine the challenge from a context outside their own is often a lost consideration which, if it had been introduced, might have led to a much more productive mentoring experience. Highlighted in the teachers' responses are key insights to their attentiveness patterns and willingness to examine change. The added value in considering engagement styles provides for the increased sense of security for the teacher and willingness to examine the student's problem, not from a power and control view, but rather from a shared collaborative position. This approach facilitates increased teacher participation and motivation. Should the use of another engagement style become part of the instructional plan, the teacher will be less resistive. One main reason is because of the valued relationship and willingness of the consultant to adjust to the engagement style of the teacher rather than the teacher adjusting to the style of the consultant.

Consultative plans can be better considered to meet the teacher's need by examining the expanded engagement patterns. First, the consultee's expressed needs as defined by the teacher are considered upon the consultant's arrival. Second, the consultant's attentiveness to problem-solving allows the teacher a valued investment. This is followed by the additional identified needs related to the particular teacher and context as explained by the teacher. The result is a greater understanding of the problem as well as of the teacher's engagement preferences and willingness to consider change. The consultant now also has the information necessary to match the client's defined communication patterns with a worldview expressed in a manner that is consistent with the consultee's style. Bergin[16] asserts that situational approaches tend to focus on environmental factors, which here allows for interactions to be developed in a manner that is in line with the consultee's engagement style communication.

Conclusion

Incorporating the prompt-scripted LIBRE Model allows the teacher and consultant a basic introduction and exchange from which they can organize and evaluate the challenge. The problem-solving process allows opportunity for the teacher to self-identify need, particular information and other resources that should be considered in processing the student's problem behavior. In addition, engagement style information offers a robust view to the complexity of the individual-in-need, including contextual and concomitant factors, which may have escaped attention in directly addressing the concern at hand. Individuals who focus on personalized interests tend to focus on enduring preferences.[17] Thus, by identifying the teacher's engagement style, a greater and deeper ecological-behavioral understanding can be processed. Bandura[18] explains the notion as agency, propositions, and schema in functional relationship with other propositions and schemata. Here the teacher's relations to self, self-expression, and oneself-awareness become added elements for consideration. The level of communication and initial exchange set the stage for how the consultant will process any change and any learning that may need to occur for a successful resolution to the identified problem. Strong rapport established early on in a consultative relationship will lead to more efficacious achievement.

Finally, problem-solving skills are learned directly by watching others as opportunity and experience avails. Problem-solving always involves a challenge, whether because of unavailability of information, limited self-confidence, lack of knowledge or access to data, prior experiences, or because a problem is not addressed or is unexpected. Eccles[19] found that cognitive performance and success expectancy is predictive of success and failure. The LMSF offers one method for collecting this information and facilitating both instruction and experience. With engagement styles incorporated into the consultation, consultant efficiency and effectiveness are exponentially increased and increased levels of rapport are possible for the teacher and consultant. Ultimately, the increased personal investment (extended through the problem-solving consultation) introduces an increased willingness and readiness to invest in the resolution.

NOTES

1. Reproduced by Permission of The DiaLog: Journal of the Texas Educational Diagnosticians Association.
2. Frederic J. Medway, "Causal attributions for school-related problems: Teacher perceptions and teacher feedback," *Journal of Educational Psychology* 71 (6), (1979): 809–818; F. Medway and J. Updyke, "Meta-analysis of consultation outcome studies," *American Journal of Community Psychology* 13, (1985): 489–504.
3. T. Santangelo, "Collaborative problem solving effectively implemented, but not sustained: A case for aligning the sun, the moon, and the stars," *Exceptional Children* 75 (2), (2009): 185–209.
4. T. B. Gutkins, "Moving from behavioral to ecobehavioral consultation: What's in a name?" *Journal of Educational and Psychological Consultation* 4, (1993): 95–99.
5. Albert Bandura, *Social Foundations of Thought and Action: A Social Cognitive Theory* (Upper Saddle River, NJ: Pearson Education Prentice Hall, 1986).

6. W. P. Erchul and T. G. Chewning. "Behavioral Consultation from Request-centered Relational Communication Perspective," *School Psychology Quarterly* 5, (1990): 1–20; J. E. Gonzalez, J. R. Nelson, T. B. Gutkin and C. S. Shwery, "Teacher Resistance to School-based Consultation with School Psychologists: A Survey of Teacher Perceptions," *Journal of Emotional and Behavioral Disorders* 12 (1), (2001): 30–37.

7. D. Funch, I. S. Funchs, M. W. Bahr, R. Fernstrom and P. M. Stecker. *Prereferral Intervention: A Prescriptive Approach* 56, (1990): 493–513.

8. P.R. Mask, "Expanding the Role of Educational Diagnosticians and School Psychologists in the Response to Intervention (RTI) Model," *The Dialog Journal of the Texas Diagnosticians' Association* 39 (2), (2010): 4–8.

9. Norma S. Guerra, "LIBRE Model Stick Figure (Revised)," Unpublished Instrument (2004).

10. Norma S. Guerra, "LIBRE Model Stick Figure," Unpublished Instrument, (2003); Norma S. Guerra, "Revised LIBRE Model Stick Figure," Unpublished Instrument (2005).

11. S. Hidi and D. Berndorlf, "Situational Interest and Learning," in *Interest and Learning: Proceedings of the Seeon Conference on Interest and Gender*, edited by L. Hoffmann, A. Krapp, K. Renninger and J. Baumert (Kiel, Germany: IPN, 1998: 74–90).

12. S. Hidi and J. M. Harackiewicz, "Motivating the Academically Unmotivated: A Critical Issue for the 21st Century," *Review of Educational Research* 70 (2), (2000): 151–179.

13. Albert Bandura, "Social Cognitive Theory: An Agentic Perspective," *Annual Review of Psychology* 52, (2001): 1–26.

14. Norma S. Guerra, "The LIBRE Problem Solving Model: A Practical Approach to Problem Solving and Decision-making for Teachers and Teacher Educators," *Texas Teacher Educator's Forum* 29, (2006): 9–14.

15. Norma S. Guerra, "LIBRE Model: Engagement Styles in Counseling," *Journal of Employment Counseling* 44, (2007): 2–10; Norma S. Guerra, Belinda B. Flores and Lorena Claeys, "A Case Study of an Induction Year Teacher's Problem Solving Using the LIBRE Model," *New Horizons in Education, Journal of Education* 57 (1), (2009): 43–57; Jeremy R. Sullivan, Peggy P. H. Hsieh, Norma S. Guerra, Christine A. Lumadue and Maritza Lebrón-Striker, "Getting Everybody Involved: A Collaborative Training Approach for Counselors and Educators," *Journal of Creativity in Mental Health* 2 (3), (2006-2007): 29–49.

16. David A. Bergin, "Influences on Classroom Interest," *Educational Psychologist* 34, (1999): 87–98.

17. M. Mitchell, "Situational Interest: Its Multifaceted Structure in the Secondary School Mathematics Classroom," *Journal of Educational Psychology* 85, (1993): 424–436.

18. Albert Bandura, *Self-Efficacy: The Exercise of Control* (New York: Freeman, 1997).

19. Jacquelynne Eccles, "Expectancies, Values and Academic Behaviors," in *Achievement and Achievement Motives*, edited by J. T. Spence (San Francisco: W.H. Freeman, 1983).

Chapter 14

Reflection

Sustaining Success

We look forward as a means to embrace and affirm the human experience.

Objective: To review problem-solving and engagement styles in care for self and others.

Let's revisit that moment when you first opened this book, with the opportunity to self-reflect and examine self with the purpose of examining your PDP. Our unifying goal: to be the best mental health service providers and client-data managers. This motivation continues with our reaffirmation that professional identity and success almost always link with attentive engagement and personal self-management. Calibrating our engagement styles to best meet the needs of the clients is one such self-regulatory commitment we make. We examined the importance of monitoring client change as contextualized in social systems with the 3Cs: cognition, culture and chronological age. We have addressed client preparation, the importance of client background information and the consideration of human growth and development both chronologically and/or as a social cognitive experience. We have discussed the CMA and LIBRE Model problem-solving exchange as the conduit for collecting client data and monitoring attentiveness. Engagement and engagement styles have been discussed and the utilitarian significance of collecting and managing formative and summative data.

The entire chapter is a reprint of Guerra, N. S., & Carrillo-Bollinger, E., Engagement Styles in Consultation: The LIBRE Model Problem-Solving Tool, Volume 40, number 1, Spring 2011, 4–8. *Source:* Reproduced by permission of *The DiaLog: Journal of the Texas Educational Diagnosticians Association*.

Core to our self-reflection was Bandura's[1] human agency four core properties of identity development, which include intentionality—goal development and the plans to execute those plans; forethought—cognition associated with future goals and plan development; self-reactiveness—one's self-regulation of plans, thoughts, and goals; and self-reflectiveness—one's self-efficacy in planning and execution. We discussed the problem-solving CMA as help to contextualize the complexity of the human experience. The ecological contextual system information provided insight into individuals within their worldviews. We now have an understanding of the CMA as a shared partnership that is client contextualized to address mental health services. This service goal includes the clients' scaffolding of short-term interventions to learn new skills (growth) and long-term interventions (development) toward positive self-management. With each session, we teach clients how to normalize (and internalize) mental health gains, to monitor the new skills and invest in sustaining these positive changes. Personalized resiliency investments were developed. The ZPD approach would suggest that all (who have the cognitive capacity) can learn with scaffold support and positive change can improve troublesome situations. We used strategies to empower client change and ongoing plans for sustaining success using problem-solving as that built-in approach.

Problem-solving is that foundational guide. The LIBRE Model problem-solving activity becomes a takeaway tool that can be used for future planning to sustain professional growth and development. The social cognitive information provided a picture of the self-defined individual and we examined the client in the midst of goal-setting plans and resolution changes. We became most aware of this theme of change. Change cannot be escaped. Our shared often unstated reality is that all living beings experience change.

One final word must be communicated. Our mental health service role involves change: normalizing challenge and change toward positive client interactions. This time we look forward as a means to embrace and affirm the human experience. Adjust your engagement investment to serve as a model and to match the accomplished work. The CMA set the structure for your counseling. With your homework completed, you are now ready to work with your client. Make sure that this session is set-up to provide your client his most positive self-reflective choices. This may require you to incorporate safety nets to assist the client with decision-making actions. As before, this is information that you will have developed, but you won't present it to the client unless required. Ideally during the time you and the client have had working together, the client and you have identified and set-up safe external resources (this may be developed with your assistance through Socratic questions). This resiliency plan confirms the data you collected and the good work accomplished as your client moves forward to a positive self-managed resiliency.

The CMP was your repository for all written and recorded materials. Formative evaluation goals facilitate the acquisition of each subsequent skill leading to the larger skill. Presenting and reviewing your data with the client assists may likely increase personal efficacy skill acquisition (as you provide the positive feedback). You maintained the data for him. He is able to see his gains and challenges as expressed in his own words. Intentionality and forethought have been set up as formative evaluations. The shared overall evaluating summative measures provide points of closure. For example, you and your client work on time management. The summative goal evaluated is time management; you have this goal in place and he has been planning now for a number of weeks. You watched (and evaluated) your client's skill develop as he fills in his calendar in a day planner. This exercise captured both as formative day-to-day practice and as overall weekly time management plan. You selected to practice time management by completing a series of calendar plans before beginning the evaluation discussion. Working with the client, you affirm (modeling self-talk) the time management planning and (speaking aloud with open-ended questions) assisted in filling in any missing information. Formative (ongoing) and summative (culminating) evaluations are important self-assessment adjustment skills. You want to make sure your client has them and has learned time management under different contexts. You created and established a history of time management proficiency. Together you both invested time in the development of this skill. Interventions included problem-solving, role-play, modeling, and practice. Together, you invested in this intervention plan. Accordingly, you want to ask your client to self-evaluate his time management skills.

Together you created some evaluation criteria: Is the information specific enough to be completed? Is this a realistic plan? Am I committed to this plan? Will the subgoals assist me in the future to benchmark my success? What external resources do I have that can provide me feedback about my time management?

Helpful external resources for the resilience plan can facilitate the process of positive change. Thus, a nagging mother may not be included as a healthy positive resource (although this too remains unstated). Rather as a clinician you are looking for mechanisms that can be used by your client to implement positive change and to make sure that they stay on track. Positive learning is always a value to be embraced. As you work with your client, you want to make sure that he sees the confidence you have in him. Finally, in terms of self-reactiveness and self-reflectiveness, you want to make sure that your client is willing to embrace an inward view of self and has the courage to self-examine personal thoughts and efficiency and effectiveness.

Reflection

Have I taught my client how to care for self and others? Have I introduced the importance of internal self-talk and external talk from others to meet identified plans? Have we discussed the importance of positive external persons? Does my client have the resiliency and protective factors (supportive friends, family, or others) to stand up and go forward?

Yours to ponder and to respond.

Clinician Self-Reflection

Let's step away from the client to consider the same questions for self. How would I respond to these same questions and offer evaluative feedback to myself? Do my personal and professional thoughts help me? Professionally, am I as efficient and effective as I can be? When all is going well, how do I encourage myself? This becomes your opportunity to reflect upon your own PDP. Reviewing my clients' CMAs and CMPs, which include the administered LIBRE Model problem-solving exchanges and calibrated engagement styles, what social cognitive life span and cultural data did I collect? How did I incorporate that information into the case plan (with each client)? This may be the perfect time for you to come back to the LIBRE Model to process how I changed. Where am I now? You create the problem-solving experiences for yourself.

Return to the Client

The importance of ongoing data collection with background questions about how best to work with different age groups is a major component of the CMA. The CMA intends to enhance your clinical practice by acknowledging your engagement role as having calibrated skills to assist your client. As a novice clinician, you were provided an ongoing rubric to measure and monitor not only your clients' success, but also your own. So let's return to review the CMA in a brief presentation.

The CMA provided you a structure to detail and facilitate client growth and social development. You began by preparing yourself, then moved into preparing to see your client. You created background questions, more questions than you ever were able to ask, but those questions were the initial groundwork you used to prepare for seeing your client. You administered the LIBRE Model problem-solving activity in the first meeting with your client. The problem-solving exchange provided you initial and sustained attentiveness information and the client's initial engagement style. You quickly collected social cognitive information about your client's environment, person and behavior, and you learned your client's goal orientation. All of this information was maintained within the CMP. You observed the problem through your client's eyes. This data was used to begin setting-up your plan. With each session you came with a defined agenda. From the data collected, you created your case plan and intervention. Evaluation measures were established with each sub-goal (formative evaluation) and goal (summative evaluation). By the end of the experience, you and your client experienced an authentic time together; one of which was strength-based, data-driven, and which introduced self-regulated change. You closed with a customized resilience plan that affirmed your client's autonomy and skill in identifying positive support and resources as future need arises.

The Human Experience as Change

You allowed the client to see the importance of change and you provided the safety net (scaffold support) for personal self-reflection. You walked with your client and normalized and monitored his or her initiated change. The CMA is used to problem solve, to monitor the client's self-care and to manage the client's gains. You, the clinician, and your client processed engagement with each meeting to address the client's need from a social cognitive and goal-oriented investment. Together change was discussed, processed and reflected upon to provide a great appreciation for the human experience.

Now with the close of your time together, you review with your client his progress and together created the resiliency plan. You are ready to part. He is empowered to go forward with the LIBRE Model problem-solving tool that can be implemented at any time or place. Your client has an increased self-awareness and the LIBRE Model problem-solving tool to monitor and track changes. This could not have been achieved had you and your client not invested the time together to maximize the shared working relationship. The CMP allowed you the opportunity to share the changes with the client. Gains had occurred and are on track to be sustained.Your work is complete and you offer yourself a positive self-statement: Good job! I remained engaged in my client's world to facilitate her positive change!

NOTE

1. Albert Bandura, "Toward a psychology of human agency," *Perspectives on Psychological Science* 1 (2006): 164–180.

Glossary of Case Management Terms

Actual engagement: style of attentiveness observed as a strong initial and sustained investment.

Attention switching: shifting from one engagement style to another as appropriate to an assessed social context.

Calibration: clinician engagement style adjustment to match or better provide client services.

Client development: life span self-regulatory interventions designed to promote personal growth and healthy positive self-regulated development.

Client growth: life span essentials to engage clients in authentic communication toward change.

Case management approach (CMA): an organizing structure for tracking the client's identified social context, goals, and engagement style orientation, in which the information is used to monitor client-clinician communication; The CMA includes: (1) Clinician self-assessment and calibration, (2) Referral and Client preparation, including clinician background work, (3) First session client meeting and administration of the problem-solving activity, (4) Data analysis and case plan generation, (5) Review of collected problem-solving units of information, which includes client identified challenges, risks, and personal strengths and resolution, (6) Intervention, (7) Intervention Evaluation, which includes criteria and measures to monitor change, and (8) Resiliency Plan, which includes follow-up, questions to develop and monitor self-managed resiliency.

Case management portfolio (CMP): overarching case folder used to structure and to track the CMA counseling sessions, client growth, monitoring, and self-regulated positive change; the components include: (1) Case Management Portfolio Table of Contents, (2) Referral, (3) Case Management Approach Form, (4) Tables of Change over Time, (5) Resilience Plan, and (6) Summary.

Case plan: identifies necessary support as a statement used to frame the services provided; orients the intervention for the clinician to develop goals and plans that will allow the client to go forward and adapt accordingly to a predetermined plan.

Congruency: being genuine and agreeable in how you present yourself.

Ecosystem: factors that do not directly involve the individual, but have a significant influence on the individual.

Engagement: an observable behavioral manifestation of initial and sustained attentiveness.

FERPA: Family Educational Rights and Privacy Act; federal law that ensures the privacy of students' education records.

Forethought: goals and projected outcomes to guide and motivate intentionality.

Formative evaluation: monitors smaller changes that are assessed in an ongoing manner.

Goal-focused engagement: style of attentiveness observed as a limited initial engagement with a strong sustained investment.

Goal orientation: a motivational or movement investment in which the individual is engaged in achieving the focal activity or task.

Intentionality: formation of plans and strategy development.

LIBRE model: Listen-Identify-Brainstorm-Reality-test-Encourage problem-solving activity that can be used as a brief therapeutic intervention or as a tool to monitor or gauge change.

LIBRE model stick figure tool (LMSFT): Listen-Identify-Brainstorm-Reality-test-Encourage graphic organizer that accompanies the LIBRE Model problem-solving exchange and functions as a clinical instrument to record problem-solving responses.

Macrosystem: an umbrella influence that affects all of the other systems and accounts for much of the individual's social, cultural, economic, religious, and political views.

Mesosystem: the connection and interactions between, among, and beyond microsystems.

Metacognition: conscious awareness of one's thinking.

Microsystem: individual's immediate environment that functions as a nested cup of interactions between the individual and the environment.

Potential engagement: style of attentiveness observed as a limited initial and sustained investment.

Professional development: pre- and practicing professional investment that involves learning and refining specialized skills consistent with identified ethical standards.

Referral: introductory materials provided to the service provider prior to receiving a client; included are the client's name, age, background, and other pertinent information.

Risk-management plans: addresses what to do when faced with crisis or potential crisis or anticipated challenges.

Self-congruency: being true to yourself.

Self-efficacy: how you see yourself in relation to the identified task established as a goal.

Self-reactiveness: selection of appropriate self-regulated choices and actions for the completion of identified plans.

Self-reflectiveness: a metacognitive process involving self-examination of personal thoughts and efficiency.

Self-regulation: self-management, including both cognitive and affective variables.

Social cognitive theory: a reciprocal relation between the individual, behavior, and environment, which interact to determine or influence one's behavior, environment, and person.

Summative evaluation: the monitoring of larger goal changes, particularly at the closing of client progress.

Tables: tabular representations of client or other pertinent information that is being tracked over time; tables are found within the CMP.

Venting engagement: style of attentiveness observed as a strong initial engagement with a limited sustained investment.

Zone of proximal development (ZPD): socially mediated process, which asserts that learning, is a centrally structured activity involving supportive language interactions.

3Cs: represents the variables of chronological age, culture, and cognition that should be identified when setting up for the first session and monitored over the course of providing client services.

Bibliography

American Counseling Association. 2014. ACA code of ethics. http://www.counseling.org/resources/aca-code-of-ethics.pdf.

American Psychological Association. 2010. Ethical principles of psychologists and code of conduct. http://www.apa.org/ethics/cod/index.aspx.

Anderman, Eric M., Chammie C. Austin, and Dawn M. Johnson. 2002. The development of goal orientation. In *Development of Achievement Motivation*, edited by Allan Wigfield and Jacquelynne S. Eccles, 197–220. San Diego: Academic Press.

Anderson, John R. 1993. Problem solving and learning. *American Psychologist* 48 (1): 35–44.

Appleton, James J., Sandra L. Christenson and Michael J. Furlong. 2008. Student engagement with school: Critical conceptual and methodological issues of the construct. *Psychology in the Schools* 45 (5): 369–386.

Arredondo, Patricia. 2006. Multicultural competencies and family therapy strategies with Latino families. In *Counseling and Family Therapy with Latino Populations*, edited by Robert L. Smith and R. Esteban Montilla, 77–95. New York: Routledge Taylor & Francis Group.

Bandura, Albert. 1997. *Self-Efficacy: The Exercise of Control*. New York: Freeman.

Bandura, Albert. 1988. Self-regulation of motivation and action through goal systems. In *Cognitive Perspectives on Emotion and Motivation*, edited by Vernon Hamilton, Gordon H. Bower, and Nico H. Frijda, 37–61. New York: Kluwer Academic/Plenum Publishers.

Bandura, Albert. 2001. Social cognitive theory: An agentic perspective. *Annual Review of Psychology* 52: 1–26.

Bandura, Albert. 1986. *Social Foundations of Thought and Action: A Social Cognitive Theory*. Upper Saddle River, NJ: Pearson Education Prentice Hall.

Bandura, Albert. 2006. Toward a psychology of human agency. *Perspectives on Psychological Science* 1 (2): 164–180.

Bandura, Albert, and Dale H. Schunk. 1981. Cultivating competence, self-efficacy, and intrinsic interest through proximal self-motivation. *Journal of Personality and Social Psychology* 41 (3): 586–598.

Bergin, David A. 1999. Influences on classroom interest. *Educational Psychologist* 34: 87–98.

Bronfenbrenner, Urie and Pamela A. Morris. 2006. The bioecological model of human development. In *Handbook of Child Psychology*, 6th ed., edited by William Damon and Richard M. Lerner, 793–828. Hoboken, NJ: John Wiley & Sons.

Bronfenbrenner, Urie. 1989. Ecological systems theory. In *Annals of Child Development: Vol. 6. Six Theories of Child Development*, edited by Ross Vasta, 187–249. Greenwich, CT: JAI Press.

Bronfenbrenner, Urie. 1986. Ecology of the family as a context for human development: Research perspectives. *Developmental Psychology* 22 (6): 723–742.

Bronfenbrenner, Urie. 1970. Reaction to social pressure from adults versus peers among soviet day school and boarding school pupils in the perspective of an American sample. *Journal of Personality and Social Psychology* 15 (3): 179–189.

Bronfenbrenner, Urie. 1979. *The Ecology of Human Development: Experiments by Nature and Design.* Cambridge, MA: Harvard University Press.

Brooks, Robert and Sam Goldstein. 2003. *The Power of Resilience: Achieving Balance, Confidence, and Personal Strength in Your Life.* New York: McGraw-Hill.

Carver, Charles S., and Michael F. Scheier. 2000. On the structure of behavioral self-regulation. In *Handbook of Self-Regulation*, edited by Monique Boekaerts, Paul R. Pintrich, and Moshe Zeidner, 41–84. San Diego: Academic Press.

Chi, Michelene T. H., Robert Glaser, and M. J. Farr, Eds. 1988. *The Nature of Expertise.* Hillsdale, NJ: Lawrence Erlbaum Associates, Inc.

Christenson, Sandra L., Amy L Reschly, and Cathy Wylie, eds. 2012. *Handbook of Research on Student Engagement.* New York: Springer.

Clark, Christopher M., and Penelope L. Peterson. 1986. Teachers' thought processes. In *Handbook of Research on Teaching*, 3rd ed., edited by Merlin C. Wittrock, 255–296. New York: MacMillan Publishing Company.

Clark, Ellen R., Linda G. Jackson, and Linda Prieto. 2011. Identity: A central facet of culturally efficacious bilingual education teachers. In *Teacher Preparation for Bilingual Student Populations,* edited by Belinda B. Flores, Rosa H. Sheets, and Ellen R. Clark, 27–39. New York: Routledge Taylor & Francis Group.

Corno, Lyn. 1986. The metacognitive control components of self-regulated learning. *Contemporary Educational Psychology* 11 (4): 333–346.

Deci, Edward L., Robert J. Vallerand, Luc G. Pelletier, and Richard M. Ryan. 1991. Motivation and education: The self-determination perspective. *Educational Psychologist* 26 (3–4): 325–346.

Desautel, Daric R. 2009. Becoming a thinking thinker: Metacognition, self-reflection, and classroom practice. *Teachers College Record* 11 (8): 1197–2020.

Dillen, Annemie. 2012. The resiliency of children and spirituality: A practical theological reflection. *International Journal of Children's Spirituality* 17 (1): 61–75.

Eccles, Jacquelynne. 1983. Expectancies, values and academic behaviors. In *Achievement and Achievement Motives*, ed. J. T. Spence, San Francisco: W.H. Freeman.

Elliot, Andrew J. and Holly A. McGregor. 2001. A 2 × 2 achievement goal framework. *Journal of Personality and Social Psychology* 80 (3): 501–519.

Erchul, W. P., and T. G. Chewning. 1990. Behavioral consultation from request-centered relational communication perspective. *School Psychology Quarterly* 5: 1–20.

Erikson, Erik H. 1963. *Childhood and Society*, 2nd ed. New York: W.W. Norton.

Erikson, Erik H. 1982. *The Life Cycle Completed: A Review*. New York: W.W. Norton & Co.

Festinger, Leon. 1957. *A Theory of Cognitive Dissonance*. Stanford, CA: Stanford University Press.

Figley, Charles R. 1986. Trauma stress: The role of the family and social support system. In *Trauma and Its Theory, Research, and Intervention*, edited by Charles R. Figley, 39–54. New York: Brunner/Mazel.

Figley, Charles R., ed. 1989. *Treating Stress in Families*. New York: Brunner/Mazel.

Flores, Belinda Bustos, Ellen Riojas Clark, Norma S. Guerra, and Serafin V. Sánchez. 2008. Acculturation among Latino bilingual education teacher candidates: Implications for teacher preparation institutions. *Journal of Latinos and Education* 7 (4): 288–304.

Flores, Belinda Bustos, Rosa H. Sheets, and Ellen R. Clark. 2011. *Teacher Preparation for Bilingual Student Populations*. New York: Routledge Taylor & Francis Group.

Fredricks, Jennifer A., Phyllis C. Blumenfeld, and Alison H. Paris. 2004. School engagement: Potential of the concept, state of the evidence. *Review of Educational Research* 74: 59–109.

Funch, D., I. S. Funchs, M. W. Bahr, R. Fernstrom, and P. M. Stecker. 1990. *Prereferral Intervention: A Prescriptive Approach* 56: 493–513.

Furrer, Carrie, and Ellen Skinner. 2003. Sense of relatedness as a factor in children's academic engagement and performance. *Journal of Educational Psychology* 95 (1): 148–162.

Gamezy, Norman. 1991. Resiliency and vulnerability to adverse developmental outcomes associated with poverty. *American Behavioral Sciences* 34: 416–430.

Gonzalez, J. E., Nelson, J. R., Gutkin, T. B., and Shwery, C. S. 2004. Teacher resistance to school-based consultation with school psychologists: A survey of teacher perceptions. *Journal of Emotional and Behavioral Disorders* 12 (1): 30–37.

Guerra, Norma S., Belinda B. Flores, and Lorena Claeys. 2009. A case study of an induction year teacher's problem solving using the LIBRE Model. *New Horizons in Education, Journal of Education* 57 (1): 43–57.

Guerra, Norma S. 2009. Illustrations of engagement styles: Four teacher candidates. *Teacher Education and Practice* 22 (1): 95–117.

Guerra, Norma S. 2001. LIBRE model. Unpublished manuscript.

Guerra, Norma S. 2007. LIBRE model: Engagement styles in counseling. *Journal of Employment Counseling* 44: 2–10.

Guerra, Norma S. 2003. LIBRE model Stick Figure. Unpublished instrument.

Guerra, Norma S. 2004. LIBRE model Stick Figure (Revised). Unpublished instrument.

Guerra, Norma. S. 2009. LIBRE stick figure tool: Graphic organizer. *Interventions in Schools and Clinics,* 44 (4): 1–5.

Guerra, Norma S. 2009. LIBRE stick figure tool: A graphic organizer to foster self-regulated social cognitive problem solving. *Intervention in School and Clinic* 44 (4): 229–233.

Guerra, Norma S. 2005. Revised LIBRE Model Stick Figure. Unpublished instrument.

Guerra, Norma S. 2004. The LIBRE model: A cognitive one-on-one loci approach to facilitating change. Paper presented at the Fall Teacher Education Conference, Waves of Change Consortium of State Organizations for Texas Teacher Education, Galveston, Texas.

Guerra, Norma S. 2006. The LIBRE problem solving model: A practical approach to problem solving and decision-making for teachers and teacher educators. *Texas Teacher Educator's Forum* 29 Spring: 9–14.

Gutkins, T. B. 1993. Moving from behavioral to ecobehavioral consultation: What's in a name? *Journal of Educational and Psychological Consultation* 4: 95–99.

Heider, Fritz. 1958. *The Psychology of Interpersonal Relations*. Hoboken, NJ: John Wiley & Sons Inc.

Hidi, S. and D. Berndorlf. 1998. Situational interest and learning. In *Interest and Learning: Proceedings of the Seeon Conference on Interest and Gender*, edited by L. Hoffmann, A. Krapp, K. Renninger, and J. Baumert, 74–90. Kiel, Germany: IPN.

Hidi, S., and J. M. Harackiewicz. 2000. Motivating the academically unmotivated: A critical issue for the 21st century. *Review of Educational Research* 70 (2): 151–179.

Krause, Neal. 2007. Longitudinal study of social support and meaning in life. *Psychology and Aging* 22 (3): 456–469.

Leinhardt, Gaea, and James G. Greeno. 1986. The cognitive skill of teaching. *Journal of Educational Psychology* 78 (2): 75–95.

Luthar, Suniya S., Dante Cicchetti, and Brownyn Becker. 2000. The construct of resilience: A critical evaluation and guidelines for future work. *Child Development* 71 (3): 543–562.

Mask, P. R. 2010. Expanding the role of educational diagnosticians and school psychologists in the response to intervention (RTI) model. *The Dialog Journal of the Texas Diagnosticians' Association*, 39 (2): 4–8.

Maslow, Abraham H. 1998. *Maslow on Management*. New York: Wiley.

Maslow, Abraham H. 1968. *Toward a Psychology of Being*. 2nd ed. New York: D. Van Nostrand.

Mayer, Richard E., and Merlin C. Wittrock. 2006. Problem solving. In *Handbook of Educational Psychology 2nd edition*. Mahwah, NJ: Erlbaum.

Medway, Frederic J. 1979. Causal attributions for school-related problems: Teacher perceptions and teacher feedback. *Journal of Educational Psychology* 71 (6): 809–818.

Medway F., and J. Updyke. 1985. Meta-analysis of consultation outcome studies. *American Journal of Community Psychology* 13: 489–504.

Miller, Patricia H. 2011. *Theories of Developmental Psychology*, 5th ed. New York: Worth Publishers.

Mitchell, M. 1993. Situational interest: Its multifaceted structure in the secondary school mathematics classroom. *Journal of Educational Psychology* 85: 424–436.

Murphy, Gregory L., and Jack C. Wright. 1984. Changes in conceptual structure with expertise: Differences between real-world experts and novices. *Journal of Experimental Psychology: Learning, Memory, and Cognition* 10 (1): 144–155.

National Association of School Psychologists. 2010. *Principles for Professional Ethics*. Bethesda, Maryland: National Association of School Psychologists.
National Association of Social Workers. 2008. Code of ethics. http://www.socialworkers.org/pubs/code/code.asp#.U_pTFJszeyw.gmail.
Patel, Vimla L., Robert Glaser, and Jose F. Arocha. 2000. Cognition and expertise: Acquisition of medical competence. *Clinical and Investigative Medicine* 23 (4): 256–260.
Reschly, Amy L., E. S. Huebner, James J. Appleton, and Susan Antaramian. 2008. Engagement as flourishing: The contribution of positive emotions and coping to adolescents' engagement at school and with learning. *Psychology in the Schools* 45 (5): 419–431.
Rogoff, Barbara. 1990. *Apprenticeship in thinking: Cognitive development in social context*. New York: Oxford University Press.
Santangelo, T. 2009. Collaborative problem solving effectively implemented, but not sustained: A case for aligning the sun, the moon, and the stars. *Exceptional Children* 75 (2): 185–209.
Schunk, Dale H. 1990. Goal setting and self-efficacy during self-regulated learning. *Educational Psychologist* 25 (1): 71–86.
Schunk, Dale H. 2008. *Learning Theories: An Educational Perspective*. 5th ed. Upper Saddle River, NJ: Pearson.
Schunk, Dale H. 2012. *Learning Theories: An Educational Perspective*. Boston, MA: Allyn & Bacon.
Schunk, Dale H. and Peggy A. Ertmer. 2000. Self-regulation and academic learning: Self-efficacy enhancing interventions. In *Handbook of Self-Regulation*, edited by Monique Boekaerts, Paul R. Pintrich, and Moshe Zeidner, 631–649. San Diego: American Press.
Skinner, Ellen A., and Jennifer Pitzer. 2012. Developmental dynamics of student engagement, coping, and everyday resilience. In *The Handbook of Research on Student Engagement*, edited by S. Christenson, A. Reschly, and C. Wylie, 21–45, New York: Springer Science.
Smith, Robert L. and R. Esteban Montilla. 2006. *Counseling and Family Therapy with Latino Populations*. New York: Routledge Taylor & Francis Group.
Sullivan, Jeremy R., Peggy P. H. Hsieh, Norma S. Guerra, Christine A. Lumadue, and Maritza Lebrón-Striker. 2006–2007. Getting everybody involved: A collaborative training approach for counselors and educators. *Journal of Creativity in Mental Health* 2 (3): 29–49.
Vygotsky, Lev S. 1978. *Mind in Society: The Development of Higher Psychological Processes*. Cambridge, MA: Harvard University Press.
Williams, Kipling D. 2007. Ostracism. *Annual Review of Psychology* 58: 425–452.
Zimmerman, Berry J. 2000. The development of scientific reasoning skills. *Development Review* 20: 99–149.
Zimmerman, Barry J., and Dale H. Schunk, eds. 2001. *Self-Regulated Learning and Academic Achievement: Theoretical Perspectives*, 2nd ed. Mahwah, NJ: Lawrence Erlbaum Associates Publishers.

Index

www.ingramcontent.com/pod-product-compliance
Ingram Content Group UK Ltd.
Pitfield, Milton Keynes, MK11 3LW, UK
UKHW012040150926
475560UK00001B/110

9 781442 246355